J

Thanks for being
great client & a great
"boss".

   ~signature~ 11/2012.

The **BAPKIN** Plan

The **BAPKIN** Plan

A Back-of-the-Napkin Approach to Financial Empowerment

Gerard Hass

iUniverse, Inc.
Bloomington

The BAPKIN Plan
A Back-of-the-Napkin Approach to Financial Empowerment

Copyright © 2012 by Gerard P. Hass

All rights reserved. No part of this book may be used or reproduced by any means, graphic, electronic, or mechanical, including photocopying, recording, taping or by any information storage retrieval system without the written permission of the publisher except in the case of brief quotations embodied in critical articles and reviews.

The information, ideas, and suggestions in this book are not intended to render professional advice. Before following any suggestions contained in this book, you should consult your personal accountant or other financial adviser. Neither the author nor the publisher shall be liable or responsible for any loss or damage allegedly arising as a consequence of your use or application of any information or suggestions in this book.

iUniverse books may be ordered through booksellers or by contacting:

iUniverse
1663 Liberty Drive
Bloomington, IN 47403
www.iuniverse.com
1-800-Authors (1-800-288-4677)

Because of the dynamic nature of the Internet, any web addresses or links contained in this book may have changed since publication and may no longer be valid. The views expressed in this work are solely those of the author and do not necessarily reflect the views of the publisher, and the publisher hereby disclaims any responsibility for them.

Any people depicted in stock imagery provided by Thinkstock are models, and such images are being used for illustrative purposes only.

Certain stock imagery © Thinkstock.

ISBN: 978-1-4759-4204-0 (sc)
ISBN: 978-1-4759-4205-7 (e)
ISBN: 978-1-4759-4206-4 (dj)

Printed in the United States of America

iUniverse rev. date: 9/25/2012

To my parents, Bernard and Tody. Thank you for the wonderful upbringing and loving childhood that you gave me.

Contents

Acknowledgments	ix
Disclaimer	x
Introduction	xi
Part I: The Back of the Napkin	**1**
Step 1: A Better Life	3
Step 2: Live within Your Means	12
Step 3: Time to Take Inventory	21
Step 4: Protect Yourself: Savings and Insurance	26
Step 5: Protect Your Loved Ones—Estate Planning	37
Step 6: Understand Tax Matters	51
Step 7: Have a Personal Pension Plan Strategy	64
Step 8: Have a Disciplined Investment Strategy	84
Step 9: Your Financial Adviser Is Here to Help You	99
Conclusion to Part I	107
Part II: The Whole Tablecloth	**111**
Step 1: Beyond the Napkin—A Better Life	113
Step 5: Beyond the Napkin—Protect Your Loved Ones	118
Step 7: Beyond the Napkin—Have a Personal Pension Plan Strategy	127

STEP 8: BEYOND THE NAPKIN—HAVE A DISCIPLINED INVESTMENT
    STRATEGY   148

PART III: DESSERT (APPENDICES)   **211**

APPENDIX 1: STRATEGIES—ACADEMIC AND PROFESSIONAL
        INFLUENCES   213
APPENDIX 2: THE BALANCED DIET—A FRAMEWORK FOR FINANCIAL
        DECISION MAKING AND EMPOWERMENT   220
BIBLIOGRAPHY   227

Acknowledgments

I would like to thank my good friend and management consultant, Keith Gear, and my colleagues from the past—Mr. G. Tod Wright and Mr. Christopher Pearson—for their help in reviewing the material in this book. Through the years these gentlemen have been a wonderful support group, and I greatly appreciate their contribution to the current cause. I would also like to thank my colleagues from the present—Laima Dingwall and Amanda Archibald – for their help, as well as the editorial staff at iUniverse for their excellent advice and attention to detail.

I would be remiss if I didn't thank the many professionals and academics who have had a very important impact on my life and investment knowledge. In particular—Benjamin Graham, Louis Rukeyser, Warren Buffet, John Steele Gordon, Marty Zweig, James P. O'Shaughnessy, Dr. Jeremy Siegel, William O'Neil, Pat Dorsey, Jason Zweig, and Peter Lynch. Their writings and teachings have fed my insatiable appetite for knowledge and given me infinite entertainment over the past 30 years.

To my assistant, Susan Tutko, thank you for fielding the calls when my mind wandered into the deep recesses of what used to be a memory.

Finally, this book would not have been completed if not for Michele Temple and her friendship, love, and encouragement.

Disclaimer

The BAPKIN Plan is offered by Gerard Hass in his individual capacity and not in the capacity as a registered representative of Raymond James Ltd. (RJL) or any of its affiliates and does not necessarily express the opinions of RJL. This book is provided as a general source of information and should not be considered personal investment advice. It is not to be construed as an offer or solicitation for the sale or purchase of securities. Nor should it be considered personal taxation advice. We recommend any investor seek independent advice from an investment adviser prior to making investment decisions and from a professional accountant concerning tax-related matters. This book is furnished on the basis and understanding that RJL is to be under no liability whatsoever in respect thereof.

Introduction

Just over a year ago, a good friend made the mistake of asking me what *simple* financial steps he should be taking. That question resulted in his having to endure an hour sit-down, albeit at a great restaurant, where I droned on about the minimum people should be doing regarding their personal finances. At the end of it, I had written down the basic steps to be done on the back of a napkin. For this reason, I consider this the "back-of-a-napkin" approach to financial planning—or BAPKIN planning, for short. It's an approach that can work for you.

A TD Waterhouse Financial Planning poll conducted in 2011 suggests that 61 percent of Canadians between the ages of 45 and 64 don't have a formal plan in place, even though one half of those said that they think a financial plan is necessary. Why is this? After speaking to friends, family, colleagues, clients, and a few select animals with wisdom named Teddy, James, and Kitty, I discovered four main reasons for having no financial plan:

1. The service is not offered to them by their financial adviser.
2. The clients consider it too cumbersome or intrusive a process.
3. They feel embarrassed by their perceived lack of knowledge or are overwhelmed by conflicting advice.

4. They don't see the need to have a plan as pressing and hence procrastinate going through the process.

Do you worry about the unexpected and the economic changes the entire world is experiencing? A financial plan can help, according to CNW Newswire. Though the plans themselves may not exist on paper or be pressing, each of us should have a practical framework to make financial decisions. For this reason, and my belief that we are heading to a crisis in future years, I wrote this book. I am hoping that it will serve two purposes.

First, I hope it will inspire you and provide you with a financial decision-making framework. Second, I hope you will use it as a reference guide that you can return to if you don't understand what your financial adviser is recommending you do.

Throughout this book, I've summarized the napkin scratch at the back of the chapter and have included "rules of thumb" to follow, which I've called "thumbprints." I've worked in the financial services field for 30 years as a chartered accountant, a financial planner, an educator, an investment adviser, and a portfolio manager. Through these different professional disciplines, I've dealt with hundreds of clients from all walks of life, and I've come to know that many people, regardless of their background, just want simple but effective guidance that is easy for them to follow.

I know the vast majority of you out there are interested in having a financial plan, are interested in getting financial advice, and are interested in having a better life, but you just can't be bothered or you aren't comfortable because you don't understand what others are telling you. I'm hoping these rules of thumb will enable you to make a decision that you can stick to a little easier.

After each summary of the BAPKIN scratch, I've put a summary of the steps that should be followed along with a simple question—yes or no—that you should be able to answer. If you have already addressed the step in your life, then great for you, but if no is your answer, then you know you have some work to do.

I've also included more detailed information—for those who are keeners—in a second part of the book titled "The Whole Tablecloth" so that you can explore and learn above and beyond what the BAPKIN scratch calls for, if you so desire.

You should note that while the general concepts discussed in the BAPKIN Plan can be applied by almost everyone, everywhere, certain topics, such as retirement products, income taxes, and estate issues, apply specifically to Canadians. Should anyone from around the world, including our neighbours to the south (unless you're in Alaska), happen to come across this book in their reading journey, I hope you get enough out of the basic material to still make the reading worthwhile, but you will need to get more specific information about your particular country's systems from other sources, I'm afraid.

For the sake of those who aren't going to read any further and are going to put this book back on the shelf, here's a summary of the steps that are written on the back of the napkin.

1. You'll learn how to develop a commitment to setting simple goals and to following a simple plan based on common sense. You'll develop a savings target to work toward and develop a plan to have no debt when you retire.
2. You'll learn strategies to live within your means—and that includes having a component for savings. You'll have a savings plan and goal.
3. You'll learn to draft up a statement of net worth and revisit it every year. Use it to make decisions which emphasize buying assets that are capable of appreciating and that result in reducing debt. That's how wealth grows!
4. You'll learn how to protect yourself. In addition to an emergency fund and a line of credit, there are various insurances to protect many different things that can put a wrench in your wealth-creation efforts.
5. You'll learn about how to protect your loved ones. Have life insurance coverage. Have a will and powers of

attorney. Have a list of assets, creditors, and people or institutions with whom you deal.
6. You'll learn how you are taxed and the importance of getting professional help for what you should be doing. You should have a basic knowledge of how the tax system works and how to reduce taxes using the 3 Ds and 3 Cs.
7. You'll learn a personal pension plan strategy based on your stage in life. If you don't have vast amounts of wealth, you may need to guarantee income for life.
8. You'll learn to develop a disciplined investment strategy that will suit your objectives and that you will be able to stick with. It must satisfy your emotional ability to handle volatility and risk. The focus should be on your asset mix, diversification, and making use of different investment styles. You need to have an appropriate way to measure if you're on track.
9. You'll learn how to work with an adviser—not the salesman—who is a professional. A suit or a big-name institution doesn't designate professionalism; credentials and integrity do. Think about consolidating for tax-efficiency purposes (but only if with a trusted expert) or making use of a fee-based wealth management coach.

Congratulations to those who are starting to read this book. You are taking a great stride forward in your financial empowerment by reading this material and implementing its advice. You don't need to implement all of these steps all at once; as the structure of the book suggests, they can be done one step at a time. What you need to do really isn't overbearing, you just need to say to yourself that you must do it and then get on with it. One step at a time, starting with Step 1 ...

Happy reading!

Part I: The Back of the Napkin

Step 1: A Better Life

You know you want it! The Dalai Lama says so.

My friend Michele looked up at the people gathered on the overpass along Highway 401, now appropriately named the Highway of Heroes on its stretch from Trenton to Toronto, and asked, "Why do you suppose they do it?"

I looked up as I always did, at each successive overpass, to nod my respects to the scores of people who had dedicated this Sunday afternoon to standing along the highway, some with Canadian flags waving, others with signs, and yet others with just themselves but all with a sense of purpose. Firemen in full dress uniform from each community along the route stood on fire trucks, providing colour guards with flags flying, as did some Ontario Provincial Police officers. They were here, as they always are, to pay their respects to the most recent Canadian soldier who had been killed while on duty in Afghanistan.

"I suppose they are here to pay their respects to the deceased and show love and support to his family."

"I understand that," Michele commented. "I mean, why do you think the soldiers become soldiers?"

Good question. Having spent five and a half years in the Royal Hamilton Light Infantry, I felt somewhat qualified to provide an answer. "Various reasons, I would imagine. Speaking for myself, I felt a sense of duty to serve my country and help others, I craved the adventure that the military provides, and I thought maybe I could make a difference in ensuring that democracy and freedom remained entrenched in our daily lives. I also got $18.25 a day."

Okay. So the money I got paid was very little incentive considering I made more than three times that amount as a student employee at Stelco. Michele did pose a good question though. Why would people be willing to sacrifice their lives for people they don't even know? It also got me to thinking further. What motivates us to take chances or make sacrifices for what seems to be little reward? What core needs are we trying to satisfy?

Core Desires

I know that when I ask clients what their core desires are, a common answer is that they want to reduce stress and simplify their lives. But as I question them further and we drill down to why each need is important, a common theme develops—most people express themselves as wanting to enjoy life and/or wanting to help others.

These are our core desires, and they lead to the conclusion that we are looking for our lives to have meaning. We want to feel like our existence matters. We want to feel a sense of accomplishment. We want to justify our life. We want to understand our purpose. We want to feel inner peace and have peace of mind.

Having a sense of purpose is the root of our desires, and this leads us to want a better life. That's what we are seeking. The Dalai Lama has expressed that our life's purpose is to seek happiness and that our journey is that of seeking something better. I happen to think he's right, and perhaps, upon reflection, so will you.

If we are seeking a better life, the next step is to understand the importance of our health in contributing to that goal. Oh, I'm not just talking about our physical and mental health, although these are very important components of our overall health. But you should recognize that many different facets of your life are integrated. I like to think in terms of five different facets of health—I've already mentioned mental or emotional health and your physical health—but there is also the health of your relationships, your spiritual health, and your financial health.

You may not think so, but these are all integrated, like pieces of a puzzle. If one of these components is doing poorly, it can have negative effects on the other aspects of your health.

Let me give you an example. Years ago while working as an investment adviser, I came across a couple, Diane and Henry, who had made some terrible financial choices. Henry was working for steel manufacturer Stelco Inc. and had seen the stock rise out of the recession in the early '90s from $1 a share to $9. Henry was convinced that this was only the beginning of something big, so he and his wife invested their entire retirement savings, amounting to several hundred thousand dollars, into the stock. Not very prudent. As well, Diane had power of attorney on a family member's money, and they invested all that money into Stelco stock as well.

By the time I had met the couple, the damage was done. They had several months where they could have undone their financial folly, but they wanted to score big so they sat on their investment and hoped for the best. Unfortunately the best didn't happen. Stelco stock went down significantly, and they saw more than half their savings disappear quite quickly. And it got worse. Stelco eventually went bankrupt before US Steel bought the assets, but there was nothing left for the shareholders.

The stress of having put all their money, including the money Diane was looking after for her family member, into one stock that didn't do well was taking its toll on their relationship. Diane's emotional health had deteriorated to the point where she was on antidepressants, and her physical health had also deteriorated as a result of all the worry. She was continually sick, and it affected her work.

The couple ended up eventually pulling themselves out of the financial crisis, but only because both of them had jobs with pensions. Their retirement lifestyle was significantly reduced because of their choice, and they both had to work almost a decade beyond what they had originally planned on.

Relationships, financial health, emotional health, physical health: I think that you can see from their experience just how the different pieces of the puzzle can affect your well-being.

I'm not qualified to advise on relationships, emotional health, and fitness, but these components are just as important as financial health. Someone in poor health can have difficulty earning money from employment and may have high medical bills that eat away at his wealth or make it very hard for him to create any. If you are depressed, it might have an effect on your work and creativity.

Seek out knowledge in these areas, but like everything else, keep it simple. You are more likely to stick to it if you do. For example, it's not rocket science to understand that maintaining a healthy weight will help you stay physically healthy. A proper diet combined with exercise can help control this. A person wanting to eat in a healthy manner would be sure to control portion sizes and not to overeat. He would stick to low fat items, and vegetables would not be a foreign word unless, of course, you spoke a foreign language in which case it would be some other word that meant vegetables.

Which reminds me: I personally believe that having a sense of humour and not taking yourself too seriously goes a long way to good health and happiness. If nothing else, read the comics once in awhile. Smile a lot and thank people even for the smallest things. A positive attitude can help you take the right steps to making your dreams a reality.

Being Committed to a Better Life

So, you've concluded that you also are seeking a better life. What is the first financial step that you should be taking?

The first step is to be committed to following a simple plan with a simple goal, something that you can remain committed to without it being overbearing. We'll start with Step 1: being motivated, committed, and having a target number. A what? A target number.

C'mon, you must have seen the commercials that some financial institutions have been sponsoring telling you that you're supposed to have a personal number.

The target number is what you are striving for your investment assets to be worth at retirement. It must be achievable based on your personal circumstances, and for most people it will fall between $300,000 and $900,000. I also like clients to have a second target number, a higher number that includes the value of your home and any other assets that can be sold to provide retirement income or a value for an estate. This second number helps us make big-picture financial decisions throughout our lives, but we'll touch on this later.

Middle-aged, middle-class workers are kidding themselves if they feel they are going to have a retirement as comfortable as their parents without saving for it. The reason is that many of our parents had defined-benefit pension plans. These are the type that most teachers, health care workers, and government workers have. They are guaranteed incomes that are paid to them in retirement based on their years of service and the income levels they earned.

According to data provided by Statistics Canada for 2008, about 30 years ago almost 35 percent of the labour force belonged to a defined-benefit pension plan. No longer. Now, only about 25 percent of employees have them, and almost 60 percent of those are public sector employees. The rest of the working masses have a form of savings plan that their employer offers and provides some small contribution toward, or they have nothing at all.

While government pension programs—Old Age Security and the Canada Pension Plan (Quebec Pension Plan in Quebec)—will carry part of the load, the vast majority of workers today are responsible for saving most of the funds that go into their savings plans, and they carry all the risk of how the investments perform.

But most people are not sophisticated enough to handle these moneys in the way a pension manager would, and they lack the coolheaded needed to do so, which makes it likely that they'll earn significantly lower returns than their parents' plans did, and thus they'll have less capital to provide for them in their retirement.

There's some debate as to how much is enough, but according to a well-known pension expert a typical couple should do just fine in retirement if they pay off their house and each partner accumulates $200,000. He stated that a $500,000 RRSP, along with government money, is enough to provide a couple earning $100,000/year with what they're used to in retirement. And thus, for most middle-class persons that do not have a defined-benefit pension plan, $500,000 is a good target number to have in savings.

Of course, $500,000 is for someone who is retiring today. If you are younger, then you'll need a larger number, because costs rise over time. We can only hope that incomes also rise so that you can sock away a larger amount more easily.

Suggested target numbers based on your age and desired lifestyle:		
Current Age	$25,000 "pension"	$40,000 "pension"
60	$300,000	$700,000
50	$400,000	$900,000
40	$500,000	$1,000,000
30	$650,000	$1,200,000
Assumes 2.5% inflation rate.		

A 2010 analysis done by Russell Investments also substantiates $500,000 as a decent number to be shooting for. The study finds that you'll need to save $20 for every $1 in pension income shortfall that you would like to earn. This number is a rule of thumb that they have devised, and it incorporates the retirement needs that we may have to cover—essential living expenses and lifestyle expenses—as well as income that we may be receiving from the government or our company pension plan.

What are your retirement expenses?

Essential living expenses. These are costs that aren't going to go away. Food, shelter, transportation, health care, and utilities are examples.

Lifestyle expenses. These are costs that you will incur to live the type of lifestyle that you want to live. Trips, golfing, dinners out each month—these are the types of expenses that you don't have to incur if you don't want to or can't afford to.

Estate value. This is the capital that you want remaining when you pass away in order to provide for your loved ones. This is a personal decision, but experience has taught me that we change our minds as we age, with the emphasis on wanting to leave a greater estate as we get older.

👍 THUMBPRINT

Do a quick calculation using this modified Retirement Funding Equation:

(Essential expenses + Lifestyle expenses − CPP(QPP) − Old Age Security − Company pension) x 20.

Example:

You figure you'll need $18,000 to cover your essential living expenses and $20,000 to cover your lifestyle expenses, for a total of $38,000 in annual expenses; you estimate that you'll receive $9,000 from the Canada Pension Plan and $6,000 from Old Age Security; and you have no defined-benefit company pension plan. The math works as follows:

> 18,000 essential living expenses
> +20,000 lifestyle expenses
> −9,000 Canada Pension Plan
> −6,000 Old Age Security
> =23,000 total yearly expenses x 20
> **= $460,000 minimum savings required**

Yes I am very aware that having such a number is not as good as sitting down with a financial planner and having a proper plan prepared for you based on your personal situation, but the purpose of the BAPKIN approach is to recognize that many, many people are not going to do so. I would sooner see you doing something as simple as the napkin plan suggests rather than nothing at all. After all, if you try to achieve $500,000 in retirement savings and fall short, you'll still likely be better off than if you procrastinated and did nothing.

What should your number be? I think you need to consider your personal circumstances. How much money do you presently make? Are you comfortable with this? If you had no debts, would you be comfortable with one half that amount? My experience has been that most people would be. So a family making $140,000 would be trying to have a retirement income of $70,000.

Is this possible? Well, yes it is. It is very possible. Let's say both the husband and wife worked, with one earning $100,000 and the other earning $40,000, and they are aged 40. Let's also say that they have managed to save $80,000 in their RRSPs and company savings plans.

Since they are both working, it is reasonable to assume that, as a family unit, they could receive government pensions of about $25,000. Currently a full Canada Pension pays in excess of $10,000, and Old Age Security pays in excess of $6,000, so given that a couple could receive as much as $32,000, I think an estimate of $25,000 is being reasonable.

Could be more or less, but if they did receive $25,000 they would need to have enough capital to generate an additional $45,000 in income. Using the Russell rule of thumb of 20x, that would mean they would need to save $900,000. Assuming they save for 25 years (to age 65) and earn 4 percent on their savings, they would need to save approximately $16,500 per year combined, or just less than $1,400 per month. This would include what they and their employers are paying into their company group retirement plans. This is absolutely doable for persons dedicated to a better life, considering that, in our example, this couple would be receiving almost $9,000 per month in after-tax income while working.

The math is no different for a single person and is also achievable. After all, a single person is more accustomed to living off her sole income throughout her working years. If we are trying to achieve about 50 percent of our present income when we get to retirement, a single person would likely have a lower retirement savings goal (since it's based on a single income), and so the amount required to provide that income isn't likely as much as a married couple.

It is sometimes easier for a single person—whether a single parent or not—to save for retirement than it is for a married couple, at least once the kids have grown up and moved out, because that person need only be disciplined for himself or herself. Sometimes couples have the additional complication of one of them being a big spender.

But don't get wigged out by all these numbers. *Just decide on a target number that you are shooting for—higher or lower than $500,000.* That's a start. You can always refine it later using the help of a professional financial planner, but at least it is something that you can start to work toward right now.

BAPKIN scratch:

Be committed to a simple plan and a simple number.

Be committed to wanting a better life, and start taking steps toward better health and wealth.

Whether it is an exercise program, better eating habits, or developing a savings program, take smaller steps until you get comfortable and develop good habits. Actions take time to become habits so do things in stages until they become habits, and then take the next step. It's all about developing and sticking to a positive program, so don't derail yourself by making it too hard to do. Be proud of your small victories and learn to think positively. Decide on what your number is going to be, between $300,000 and $900,000, and start thinking about how you are going to achieve it.

I have a target number that I am saving toward: Yes No

STEP 2: LIVE WITHIN YOUR MEANS

So now that we have our "number," how do we get to it?

One critical element of the BAPKIN Plan: You should not have any debt when you retire. Simplifying life means not having to worry about payments at a time when you are relying on capital to live. No mortgage. No car loan. No debt. Debt repayment is part of the next step in the BAPKIN approach.

We supposedly live in different times than the past three decades. It is being called the "new normal," a term popularized by Bill Gross of investment management firm PIMCO, and its meaning has morphed into people no longer being voracious consumers and investment risk-takers but rather cautious, subdued, and net savers, similar to those who survived the Great Depression. It is a function of the recession and high unemployment levels that are being experienced as a result of the global financial meltdown and the aftershocks that have been occurring in economies worldwide since 2008.

> **The "new normal" from an investment perspective**
>
> The new normal also refers to investors now caring about the return *of* their capital more than the return *on* their capital. Is this a short-sighted phenomenon or something that's here to stay?

If we're not working, we're not spending. If we think our jobs might be going to disappear, we don't spend. If our new job pays less than our old job, we don't spend as much. We'd rather pay down existing debt than incur more debt. We have games nights at home and eat in a lot more. In other words, we are learning to live within our means. That's the new normal—or so that's what is supposed to be happening.

Is it? For many responsible persons, yes it is, but there is an element of society known in investment circles as the "new abnormal" or the "schizophrenic consumer." This being avoids brand name staples for items such as shampoo and toothpaste but splurges on more expensive discretionary items that he doesn't need, like a daily latte. It's sort of a Jekyll-and-Hyde spending pattern.

It seems that spending and consumption are bad habits that many find hard to break. Why? For some people, it is how we feel good about ourselves and, one would conclude, what makes us feel like we are having a better life. Unfortunately, we sometimes buy on impulse, we have trouble determining the difference between needs and wants, and we spend without considering that we need to save some of what we earn.

Well, if that person is you, my friend, that is about to change, because the next step in the BAPKIN approach is to establish a savings program and to learn to control your spending. This step is very important. It is the foundation for creating wealth. If you don't save, you won't have wealth unless you win a lottery or get a large inheritance. *You have to do this.*

I believe this to be the hardest step. It is more difficult because we live in a time where automatic payments, credit cards, and debit cards are the means with which we pay for items. It is very easy to charge items on credit cards without keeping track of the amount that we have run up. Then when the monthly statement comes in, we realize just how little control we may have had. It doesn't help that we also use debit cards, which make our task more difficult, because we don't see our account balance after each purchase so we lose track of our spending. With no immediate accountability to our spending patterns and with a bias to deny ourselves very little, we spend beyond our means or squander what could otherwise be savings.

So how do we start a savings program?

The Gung-Ho System

Some people like to record keep. Most do not. If you can't figure out where your money goes then perhaps you need to keep tabs on your spending to see if you need to make changes in your lifestyle. Note that, at first, you shouldn't change your spending habits and you shouldn't draw up a budget. Instead, you should record where it is all going for several months. There are computer programs available, such as Quicken, that will let you record your expenses easily, but you can also use an Excel spreadsheet or even go old school and keep track of your expenditures with a pad and pencil.

Summarizing these expenses for a period of time is the only way you are going to truly understand your spending habits. A personal Statement of Cash Flow summarizes all the sources from which you receive money and all the amounts that you pay out each month. I've included a sample in Figure 2-3. The net difference between the income and expenses is either savings (congratulations!) or a deficit (drat!).

Once you understand your spending patterns, the next step is to decide where you can change or curb them in order to have savings remaining. This step is known as budgeting. There are two types of expenses: *essential needs*, such as food and hydro, and *lifestyle expenses*, such as that latte that you enjoy every morning. When scaling back spending, start with lifestyle expenses. Once you have numbers that you can work with, you are tasked with spending no more than your budgeted amounts. The battle between current expenditure and future expenditure is ongoing. You'll need to learn to curb some of your desires while in savings mode.

I can recall my budget in my mid-twenties when I first moved out of my parents' house. Friends, reviewing my budget, laughed when I suggested I could cut back on haircuts and use just one lightbulb in the fixtures rather than two. Nature has taken care of the hair for me, but I felt as though it was a legitimate approach to my living within my means even if my budget suggested that I lived life on the verge of poverty. Never did reduce those haircuts, but I managed instead to curb the number of times I went to bars and ate out. I learned to appreciate reading a book on a Saturday night, although I think my lighting was insufficient and harmed my sight.

If you are already spread thin when it comes to reducing lifestyle expenditures, then perhaps, if you are capable, you will need to consider increasing your revenue. Options available include taking on a part-time job, upgrading your education at night school or online courses in order to be eligible for a better job, and asking for a raise.

You don't have to do this step alone. A professional planner would be happy to sit down with you and help you to develop a budget. If you feel there are no areas where you can cut back and you find yourself spending more than you make, then you need to see a credit counsellor.

The Envelope System

Back in my youth, my mother used to take two weeks' worth of budgeted expenses for things like groceries out of the bank account and put the money into various envelopes so that she had better control over family spending. Doing such an exercise works wonders for knowing how much you are spending and providing some control to it. As you see the money dwindle in the envelope, you start to make tough spending decisions so that it lasts until the next payday. This is known as having timely feedback in the business world.

Alas, we live in a different time now and, as mentioned before, debit and credit cards rule how we transact each day. Accepting this, I use envelopes this way: I make use of credit card purchases for most of the items that I need to track as business expenses for income tax purposes, and I use online banking to pay my bills such as hydro and cable. The nice thing about online banking is that you can see your account transactions and balances as you are making your bill payments. By having some idea of what the amounts are going in and out and what your current bank balance is, you are conducting an informal bank reconciliation in your mind. This will help you understand what is going on with your finances.

I will have a set amount in my mind as to how much I can spend on basic needs for that I would normally pay cash on the spot, such as groceries. I use my debit card for such purposes. If I know I'm only supposed to spend around $200 per week on groceries, I'll know immediately as I'm checking out whether or not I'm staying within my budget, and so making use of the debit card in this manner doesn't pose a danger to my budget.

I withdraw cash from my bank account either once each week or every second week for day-to-day lifestyle expenses, such as that magazine or latte or lunches. These expenses are discretionary, meaning I don't have to incur them, I want to incur them. I control these impulse spending urges by putting my money into the envelopes and allocating a certain amount, such as $20 each day. If I don't spend the full $20 one day, I can use it whenever I want. I have the daily cash allotment on me so I can always make a conscious decision on how I want to spend my money each day. I love using envelopes for this because I otherwise would find myself spending more than I thought each day, especially if I relied on debit and credit cards. For larger lifestyle expenses, I move the money allocated to a savings account each payday, and because I do online banking, I can see how much is in there to spend. When I'm ready to spend it, I can do so without feeling guilty, and I can spend within the amount that I've saved.

Okay, okay. I can hear a number of you groaning that there's no way you're going to be budgeting and using envelopes, no matter how practical this approach may be. Fine. For you, and even for those of you who will make use of budgeting and spending control, I will introduce the tried and true method of "paying yourself first."

Pay Yourself First

This is not rocket science, but it does take an element of discipline, albeit a smaller amount of discipline than the other methods. On each of your paydays, pay yourself first. Go online and transfer 10 percent of your take-home pay into a separate account, be it a savings account, an account with an investment adviser, or some other vehicle.

This amount represents the amount of your current cash flow that you are not going to spend for current consumption but rather for future consumption. Do it without fail, each and every payday. You have the remaining 90 percent of your pay to spend however you so wish. Can't afford to put aside 10 percent of your income? Then you are living beyond your means. Accept it and go back to the budgeting step, or get help.

> 👍 **THUMBPRINT**
>
> Pay yourself first. On each payday, immediately transfer 10 percent (15 percent if you can afford it) of your take-home pay from your bank account to a savings account, an investment account, or some other "savings" vehicle. Make it a habit to do immediately or else set up an automatic savings plan so that you don't have to think about it and aren't tempted to spend it.

The beauty of the "pay-yourself-first" method is that it can also factor in inflation and lifestyle improvements. If you get a pay raise, you save more money. If you change jobs in order to earn a higher salary, the amount you save increases also.

You should note that 10 percent may not be enough of a savings rate to provide for your retirement if you don't have a company pension plan, which most people don't. It depends on how much you have saved to date, your age, and the rate of return you will earn on your investments. But if you have no savings discipline at this time, then it's best to start at this level. If you change your lifestyle too drastically, you are less likely to stick with the discipline.

As time goes on and you get more comfortable, perhaps your debts are paid off and you have more disposable income, then try to save a larger portion of your take-home pay. Interest rates and stock returns have demonstrated some pretty low returns in the last decade. If those low investment returns remain, then 10 percent just won't cut it. For most persons, a savings rate of 15 percent should suffice.

The table below demonstrates the effects of paying yourself first using a 10 percent and a 15 percent savings rate.

	Effects of saving 10% and 15% of take-home pay			
	10%	15%	10%	15%
Current Age	$50,000 income $340 per month	$50,000 income $500 per month	$100,000 income $600 per month	$100,000 income $900 per month
30	$386,000	$568,000	$682,000	$1,020,000
40	202,000	298,000	357,000	535,000
50	91,000	134,000	160,000	240,000
60	23,000	34,000	41,000	60,000
Assumes 5% return to age 65.				

Figure 2-1

Okay, enough for the motivation. Here's a table (Figure 2-2) that should help you figure out how much you need to save each month in order to get to your "number" that you decided on in the last chapter.

How much should I be saving?					
Here's how much you need to save each month to accumulate $100,000 by age 65.					
How old are you now?	What do you think you'll earn on your savings?				
	3%	5%	6%	8%	
25	$ 108	66	50	29	Here's the amount you'll need to save each month.
30	$ 135	88	70	44	
35	$ 172	120	100	67	
40	$ 224	168	144	105	
45	$ 305	243	216	170	Magic number $500,000? Just multiply by 5.
50	$ 441	374	344	289	
55	$ 716	644	610	547	
60	$ 1,547	1,470	1,433	1,361	

Figure 2-2

Evaluating your expenses doesn't have to be overwhelming, and there are software programs that you can buy to help you track your expenses. I know many of you will not sit down and do such an exercise, but for those of you who are interested, the next page shows a sample household cash flow statement (Figure 2-3) that you can use for budgeting purposes.

BAPKIN scratch:

Live within your means and set up a savings program. Start by saving 10 to 15 percent of your take-home pay.

So are you living within your means? Do you make more money than you spend? How do you know if that's happening? One quick way is to check your bank account each month. If you're saving each month then your bank balance will be growing. But sometimes our expenses are erratic.

To ensure you are saving money, on your payday, transfer part of your pay immediately into a savings vehicle. Alternatively, you can make use of automatic contributions with your investment adviser. You can even set up additional payment amounts on your mortgage or other loans.

I now have a system for saving in place: Yes No

Annual Household Cash Flow

Inflows

Employment income (net)	76,500	Alimony	-
Professional/business income	-	Child support	-
Company pension income	-	Rental income	-
Old age security	-	Investment income	-
Canada Pension	-	Other	-
RRIF / RRSP income	-	Other	-
$	76,500	$	-

Total cash inflows $ 76,500

Outflows

Housing		Transportation	
Mortgage	14,400	Lease / loan payments	5,800
Rent	-	Vehicle insurance	1,300
Property tax	3,000	Gas and oil	2,400
Utilities	4,800	Maintenance and repairs	1,500
Supplies	300	Parking	600
Maintenance and repairs	1,500	Public transportation	-
$	24,000	$	11,600

Food and clothing		Insurance (excluding auto)	
Groceries	8,400	Home/property	600
Restaurant and entertainment	2,200	Life	1,400
Clothing	3,000	Disability	-
Other	-	Critical illness	-
Other	-	Long-term disability	-
$	13,600	$	2,000

Debt service		Savings	
Line of credit payments	-	RRSP contributions	10,000
Loan payments	3,000	TFSA contributions	5,000
Credit card payments	-	RESP contributions	-
Other	-	Non-registered savings	-
$	3,000	$	15,000

Other expenditures			
Education - tuition, books, etc.	-	Vacations	3,100
Alimony	-	Donations	800
Child support	-	Additional income taxes	3,200
$	-	$	7,100

Total other expenditures $ 7,100

Total cash outflows $ 76,300

Excess cash (deficiency) $ 200

Figure 2-3

Step 3: Time to Take Inventory

You're committed to doing something better for yourself. You've started a savings program. Now what? It's time to look at what you have accumulated up to this point. It's time to take inventory of the good and the bad.

The Overall Picture—Your Statement of Net Worth

When we look into a full-length mirror, we can usually quickly assess whether our bodies appear overweight. After determining that we want to lose some weight, the first step is to step on a scale and see how much we weigh to start with. How else are we going to measure whether our diet and exercise program is working (other than our mirror, perhaps)?

We need to conduct a similar process to assess the health of our financial situation. So it's time for us to draft up what is called a statement of net worth, which is also known as a Household Balance Sheet. I like to think of it as a report card summarizing the decisions that you made in the past from a financial perspective. The statement sums up everything you own and everything you owe. Subtract the one from the other, and you will end up with a value that represents your worth.

Not in the sense of "what you are worth as a human being"—that is much more complicated and we all know we are priceless—but rather what you have in financial terms to provide for yourself and your family as you journey through life. The government can't provide for everyone. We need to take care of ourselves, live within our means, and provide for our future, and the best way to do that is to create a "report card" to help us in our financial and lifestyle decision making.

The goal is to see the net worth increase throughout your lifetime. You want your assets to grow and your debts to shrink. There will be times when they will not. Perhaps your investments will decline in value due to a market correction, or perhaps an emergency will occur and you will need to spend some of your savings. The changes in your net worth will serve as a guide as to whether you should be making changes to your life or lifestyle. Sometimes you just need to be patient and wait for your assets to appreciate. Other times you may need to save and invest more or reduce your spending.

If you've started with Step 1, then you have already decided on a target number that you want your retirement savings to be. Now you need to set a target for your *net worth* growth. This is the second number that I wrote about in Step 1. It's all encompassing and doesn't just cover your retirement assets. If you were a business, you would probably want to see your wealth grow by at least 10 percent per year, and this ties in nicely with our savings rate goal discussed in the previous chapter. There are different ways to grow your wealth. For instance, you can save money and invest, which will make your assets grow, or you can pay down your mortgage, or just concentrate on paying down existing loans. It's up to you to decide the best combination. Just remember, make decisions that allow your investments and assets to grow and that will reduce your debts.

Take a look at the sample Household Balance Sheet (Figure 3-1). The assets are on the left side. Assets include money you have in bank accounts, loans that are owing to you from your children and deadbeat friends, RRSP investments, tax-free savings accounts, and investments that are held outside of registered accounts. For many people, their principal residence is their largest asset throughout most of their lives. You might have other real estate investments, such as a cottage or a rental property.

> 👍 **THUMBPRINT**
>
> Your framework for making financial decisions should be based on the following:
>
> *Make decisions that emphasize buying appreciating assets or reducing your debts.*
>
> By drafting a statement of net worth and updating it each year, you will become experienced at making financial decisions that promote these two goals.

I believe that you should only include assets that are *capable* of appreciating on your Household Balance Sheet. That way, you are encouraged to make decisions that will contribute to growing your net worth, not deteriorating it. Want to buy a BMW? That's fine, but it is a depreciating asset, so it is really an expense, and you should recognize that it damages your net worth, not increases it. So if you put it on your statement, you'll have to decrease its value each year. Personally, I prefer not to show it at all. And really, who cares about most of your furniture? Do you think you're going to sell it someday? If you do, do you really think you'd get much for it? Unless the answer is yes, and a significant amount, then don't include such items.

Unlike assets, all liabilities get listed under the liability column. Debts don't magically go away—they just get worse, unless you pay them off. If you had to sell all your assets for some reason, who knows what you would get for them, but you certainly do know how much you would owe if you had to settle all your debts.

Examples of liabilities include the loan owing on your vehicle, credit card balances, the mortgage on your house, and money owing on your line of credit. Or perhaps you're that deadbeat friend, in which case you would show your loan owing on the liability side of your Household Balance Sheet.

Let's take a look at the Household Balance Sheet of a real person. Roger is a self-employed environmental adviser. His most recent statement of net worth is shown in Figure 3-1. Roger has cash sitting in a high-interest savings account of $5,000 and another $5,000 in Canada Savings Bonds. These combine to $10,000 in Cash and Short-term investments. He also has RRSP investments of $108,000 and $10,000 in a Tax-Free Savings Account. He conservatively estimates that his house is worth about $320,000. These items total to being worth just less than $450,000. He has not attributed a value to his business since he is the main asset and operates out of his home. It is unlikely that he will be able to sell the business when he retires.

Household Balance Sheet

Assets - what you own			Liabilities - what you owe		
Current					
Cash and short-term investments		10,000	Income taxes payable		18,000
Accounts receivable		-	Credit card balances		-
Other		-	Lines of credit		20,000
Other		-	Other loans or debts		-
Total current	$	10,000	Total current	$	38,000
Long-term					
RRSP investments		108,000	Car loans		4,000
TFSA investments		10,000	Mortages		147,000
Non-registered investments		-	Investment loans		-
Life insurance cash value		-	Other		-
Total financial	$	118,000	Total long-term	$	151,000
Principal residence		320,000			
Cottage		-			
Other real estate		-			
Total real estate	$	320,000			
Collectibles		-			
Other		-			
Total other	$	-			
Total assets	$	448,000	**Total liabilities**	$	189,000
Total net worth	$	259,000.00			

Figure 3-1

Being self-employed, Roger has to pay quarterly instalments for his taxes, which are $18,000 this quarter. He has a line of credit of $45,000, of which he accessed $20,000 in order to buy a boat and trailer and go on a vacation. Notice that we didn't list the boat and trailer as assets, since these are depreciating assets, and he expects to get very little for the boat should he sell it after about 10 years. His income taxes and line of credit are short term in nature, meaning that they are payable within one year. The line of credit can be repaid over a period longer than a year, provided a minimum payment is made each month, but the bank also has the right to call the loan if it so chooses so it is treated as a short-term obligation.

Roger has a mortgage on his home of $147,000 and has only $4,000 remaining on his car loan. All these amounts add up to $189,000 in liabilities.

Roger's assets total $448,000 and his liabilities $189,000. This results in a net worth of $259,000. If Roger can grow his net worth by 10 percent per year through a combination of paying down debt, saving in and out of his RRSP, and through asset appreciation, he will have a net worth of more than $650,000 when he plans on retiring in 10 years' time.

I've provided a blank Household Balance Sheet for your use in the Appendix. If you make copies, you can update it yearly to keep track of your assets and liabilities. This will help you see what is actually happening with your balance sheet, and you may find you want to make some adjustments as time goes by.

BAPKIN scratch:

Draft up a Household Balance Sheet and update it each year. Use it to measure your decision-making discipline which emphasizes spending your money on assets capable of appreciating and paying down debts.

It doesn't have to be fancy. On a sheet of paper list your assets and liabilities. It should not take you very long. Be conservative in estimating the value of assets that don't have a concrete means of valuing, such as a cottage or your personal residence.

Compare your progress once a year, but always reflect how the Balance Sheet will be impacted by each significant financial decision you make throughout the year.

I have drafted an estimate of my net worth: Yes No

Step 4: Protect Yourself: Savings and Insurance

Life doesn't always go according to plan. You need to ensure that you are protected against events that may affect your ability to save money and provide a better life for you and your loved ones. Whether you become sick or disabled, old and unable to care for yourself, or perhaps are grieving for someone you cared for deeply, there are ways to limit the financial damage from getting too far out of hand.

Being protected is a basic human need. We live in buildings to shelter ourselves from the elements, we wear hard hats and bike helmets, we brush our teeth, we make laws, we wear sunscreen, and we hire police officers. The list of how we protect ourselves is endless. We need to feel safe in order to feel comfortable, and being protected in a financial sense is something everyone needs to do. The way to achieve this protection is to have savings, a line of credit, and insurance.

Savings: The Emergency Fund

Sometimes life doesn't happen the way we plan it in big or small ways. Marriages break down, accidents happen, and jobs are lost, or maybe something good like a great buy on a boat that a friend is getting rid of is thrown onto your path. Make sure that you have access to money should something go wrong in your life or should good opportunities suddenly arrive. We refer to this as an emergency fund.

How much "emergency money" should you have access to? Pundits say anywhere from three to six months of monthly expenditures that you would normally incur. Just make sure you have an idea of how much you spend in three to six months. You usually need emergency money at a stressful time in your life, and the last thing you need is to be further stressed because you didn't plan properly. If you don't know how much to save and you want to start an emergency fund right away, just use a $5,000 to $10,000 figure. It's a start.

> 👍 **THUMBPRINT**
>
> Have three-to-six months' expenditures put away in savings, but if you are unsure how much that should be, then give yourself a $5,000 to $10,000 target until you figure it out.

Keep this money in an investment that is safe and that is easily got at, like a high-interest savings account, a cashable GIC, or a money market fund. Do not put it in investments that are locked up until a maturity date or that go up and down in value, because chances are you'll need the money when the investments are down in value or when they're still locked up. Note: Tony Soprano's hiding spot for his money, a barrel in the backyard, proved not to be a good place, and mattresses have also shown to be less desirable locations, although I am told it does add a bit of comfort and cushion.

Access to a Line of Credit

Even if you have money put aside for emergencies, you should have access to a line of credit with a bank. A line of credit serves as a preapproved loan from the bank that you can access whenever you want and in whatever amount you need, up to your approved amount, that is.

Make sure this line of credit is established before you need the money, or you might find the bank not letting you have one because, depending on the emergency, you may be considered a high risk for repayment. I know of one person who lost his job and when he tried to get a line of credit from the bank to tide him over until he could find another job, the bank said thanks but no thanks.

Some people use a line of credit in lieu of putting cash savings aside. If you use your line of credit in such as fashion, you risk digging yourself into a bigger hole depending on what the emergency is. For example, I had a client who lost her job and was unemployed and living off her line of credit for nine months. The job she finally found did not pay her as much as she had been earning previously. It took her years to pay back the debt that she incurred while she was out of work. I prefer clients to have both, money set aside for emergencies and a line of credit for flexibility purposes.

One last thing about a line of credit: it's preferable to use one that's *secured* against something like your house, cottage, or perhaps a non-registered investment portfolio. That way, the interest rate charged will be lower than if you are using an *unsecured* line of credit.

Insurance(s)

In addition to savings and a line of credit, various types of insurance can also help to provide for your protection. You'll want to make sure you have proper coverage. This includes disability insurance, house and vehicle insurance, critical illness insurance, living care insurance ... Gosh, I feel like Bubba from *Forrest Gump* describing the many ways that one can eat shrimp. I think you get my point that there are many different types of insurance protection available. These products can be complicated to understand, but I'll give you a quick rundown of the important ones that you should be aware of.

Here is a list of the main types of insurance that protect you, your well-being, and your possessions.

Insurances that protect you:
- Unemployment insurance
- Sickness and health insurance
- Disability insurance

- Lender's loan and mortgage disability insurance
- Critical illness insurance
- Long-term care insurance

Insurances that protect things:
- Business interruption insurance
- Property insurance
- Vehicle insurance

Ideally you would be able to have coverage in all relevant areas that insurance exists, but unless you are well-to-do this just is not practical. For most people, damage to our property, vehicles, and some form of disability are high-probability life events.

> 👍 **THUMBPRINT**
>
> Ask yourself: What will be the implications on my quality of life if I don't have any of these protective insurances and something goes wrong? Have a discussion about these issues with your financial coach or a trusted financial professional. Wherever possible, have as much coverage and as many types of coverage as you can afford.

Insurances That Protect You

Unemployment insurance

If you are an employee in Canada, you are likely covered under the government's *employment insurance* (EI) program which will provide you with a temporary income should you become unemployed. Self-employed persons are not automatically covered, but they can be if they wish, although it's not normally recommended, since there's no opting out of the program once a claim has been paid, and a self-employed person can't lay himself off and collect EI.

Health-care insurance

All Canadians have basic provincial government *health-care* coverage. However if you want additional health-care coverage to cover areas such as prescriptions, semi-private hospital rooms, and items such as visits to a dentist or chiropractor, then you are hopefully covered through a benefits plan at work. If you do not have such a plan, it is possible to get private coverage, but expect to pay upwards of $300 per month. It may seem expensive, but if you suddenly needed extensive dental work and frequent visits to your chiropractor, the coverage may be invaluable. Ask your financial adviser to get you quotes so that you can make your decision.

> 👍 **THUMBPRINT**
>
> Working for a company that has benefits has its benefits. The value of a benefit program should not be overlooked if you have a choice between employers.

Disability insurance

Which is more important, the chicken or the egg? If you want to continue to produce eggs, I think you would agree that it's the chicken. From an insurance perspective, property insurance insures the eggs, while disability and life insurance insure the chicken.

The likelihood of being disabled is a lot higher than most people realize. In Canada, the national disability rate in 2006 rose to 14.3 percent. If the odds of your winning a lottery were 14 percent, you would expect to win at some point if you continued to buy tickets. But being disabled is one lottery that you don't want to win, and because the likelihood of your collecting disability benefits is high, the premiums for disability insurance are correspondingly high.

Both disability and death can eliminate a source of family income, and the financial effects of this would be burdensome, but becoming disabled has the added negative that your household costs could actually increase, since there would likely be medical and care issues.

There are government disability programs available through worker's compensation, the Canada (or Quebec) pension plans, and unemployment insurance, but these amounts are seldom enough. Most working persons with benefits also have group disability insurance, but sometimes these plans only cover short time periods, such as one to two years, and fail to provide long-term disability coverage.

> 👍 **THUMBPRINT**
>
> If you have a group disability plan through work, the disability income will be tax free if you and all other employees paid the premiums, and it will be taxable if your employer paid them and didn't include them as a taxable benefit on your T4.

Before you decide to sit at a green light waiting for someone to rear-end you, recognize that disability payments aren't a gravy train. In order to encourage an insured person to get back to work, disability insurance payments are purposely kept below the amount of money you would normally receive while working. The limit is typically 67 to 70 percent of your income and other disability payments are included in this total amount. Disability payments are often capped where earnings are higher, so just because you earn $200,000 per year, don't expect to receive $140,000.

Lender's loan and mortgage disability insurance

It is usually cheaper to have a personal disability policy rather than taking the insurance offered when you get a loan or a mortgage. But not everyone gets their own disability coverage besides that offered through their employer. If you're relying on the disability benefits you have from your employment benefits plan, remember that you might not always have that job.

If you don't have your own personal disability policy and you aren't sure whether you're insurable or you don't plan on getting your own insurance, then by all means take the mortgage and loan disability insurance offered by your financial institution when you get your loan. It is simple enough to qualify and it is better you are protected. You can always opt out of it later.

Critical illness insurance

Critical illness insurance provides a lump-sum benefit to you should you be diagnosed with a critical illness that's defined in the policy and should you live beyond a required survival period. It also gives you access to assistance services to help you cope with the day-to-day challenges that are typically faced when you are diagnosed with such an illness. If there is a "return of premium" rider on your policy, you can receive part or all of your premiums back should you not become critically ill.

Typical illnesses include cancer, stroke, and heart attack but can also include items such as loss of limbs or eyesight, deafness, and even loss of speech. It's important to understand what illnesses your policy covers.

Why do you need a lump sum if you are found to have a critical illness? The money can be used for whatever you so choose. If you want to go on a vacation with your family, gift money to your loved ones, or pay for treatment not covered under regular programs, it can be done. There typically are no restrictions. God knows you deserve the freedom at that point.

Critical illness is often offered to you at the time you apply for life insurance if you are found to be in good health. If the offer is made, be sure to give it some thought.

Long-term care insurance

If you become unable to care for yourself when you get older, chances are you'll need some form of long-term care assistance to help you in your day-to-day living. This help may come in the form of staying in a long-term care facility, such as a nursing home or having home care come to you.

Either way, these costs can be quite expensive and can easily eat away at savings that you thought would last a lifetime or would otherwise have gone to your loved ones. I've known two clients who paid significant amounts for home care for extended periods. Both persons had significant savings eroded to the point where there was nothing left for their heirs.

> 👍 **THUMBPRINT**
> Obtaining long-term care insurance gets more expensive as you get older. Give serious consideration to getting long-term care coverage when you are in your late fifties to early sixties.

If you're 55 to 65 years of age, I urge you to give this insurance some serious consideration.

Insurances That Protect Things

Business interruption insurance

Business owners need *business interruption insurance* in case something happens that causes a temporary shutdown of the business, such as a fire. This insurance will pay out while you're getting back on your feet after a shutdown covered by the policy.

Property insurance

Insurance on property, such as your house, is absolutely necessary to have.

A homeowner's policy has two sections: property and liability. The property component covers the dwelling and other structures on the property (such as a shed), your belongings, and the loss of use of everything. There are two basic approaches—"specified perils," which covers risks specifically named in the policy; and "all risk," which covers perils except those specifically excluded from the policy. The broader the coverage, the more expensive the policy but it is the better value. If cost is an issue, then ask for a higher deductible.

The liability component covers any loss you may incur due to negligence. So if you don't shovel your snow and a person slips in your driveway, you may be sued and you'll be glad you've got the liability component.

> 👍 **THUMBPRINT**
> Make sure your home insurance has a replacement cost rider.

The replacement cost rider is another important component of homeowners insurance. A replacement cost rider lets you receive a settlement without a deduction for depreciation. If you do not have a replacement cost rider and you need to settle a loss, the insurance company will only pay you the actual cash value of your property, which consists of the replacement cost less an amount attributed to depreciation since the property was built or bought.

If you're looking at saving money on your property insurance, here are a few tips:

1. Ask to have a higher deductible. It will cost you more if you incur a loss since part of the money to replace is going to come out of your own pocket but you will pay lower premiums for your coverage and they can add up over the years.
2. Most insurance companies give discounts if you have working fire extinguishers and smoke detectors in your property.
3. Most insurance companies will give you a discount if you combine your property insurance and your automobile insurance with them.

Vehicle insurance

If you want to drive a car, and stay on the right side of the law, you have to have automobile insurance.

Automobile insurance covers five basic kinds of protection. There is liability insurance to protect you if you injure someone or damage his or her property in an accident, medical payment coverage to cover any medical expenses not covered by your provincial health plan and provide a small disability income if you can't work, uninsured motorist coverage to protect you if you are hit by a person who has no or inadequate coverage, collision coverage to cover repairs to your vehicle if you are involved in a collision, and comprehensive insurance to cover repairs to your vehicle if caused by most non-collision incidents, such as if your vehicle is vandalized or damaged in a storm.

It's worth shopping around for quotes. Insurance is very expensive for younger people, since statistics show younger people make more claims than other age demographics, so shopping around is a necessity for them. Money can be saved by increasing deductibles and perhaps eliminating the collision coverage on older vehicles where the replacement value is negligible. If you are a member of a professional organization, you may have group automobile insurance available and it's worth getting a quote from them. It should also go without saying: drive safely (not aggressively) and don't speed. Getting in an automobile accident or losing points from a traffic ticket can result in significant premium increases that won't go away for years.

> 👍 **THUMBPRINT**
> Consider reducing your premium by increasing the collision deductible or eliminating the collision coverage if the vehicle you are driving has a low replacement value.

BAPKIN scratch:

You need to protect yourself and your loved ones from events which can have a negative impact on your savings goals and current lifestyle. Have an emergency fund that's accessible and safe. Investigate if you have protection insurance in the key areas and get covered wherever possible and within your financial means. Have a down-to-earth discussion with a trusted professional.

Vehicle and property insurance are absolute "must haves" regardless of your financial situation. Disability insurance is also necessity. If you have plenty of spare cash flow, both critical illness and long-term care insurances are worthwhile to have for most people.

I have established an emergency fund: Yes No

Gerard Hass

I have discussed, thought about, and, where I deemed appropriate, acted on the following protections:

Unemployment insurance	**Yes No**
Health insurance	**Yes No**
Disability insurance	**Yes No**
Lender's loan and mortgage disability insurance	**Yes No**
Critical illness insurance	**Yes No**
Long-term care insurance	**Yes No**
Business interruption insurance	**Yes No**
Property insurance	**Yes No**
Vehicle insurance	**Yes No**

Step 5: Protect Your Loved Ones—Estate Planning

Perhaps one of the least desirable things to think about is our own death. But unless you're single and a recluse, chances are you have loved ones for which you are responsible and want to care for. The next area that we'll look at is how to simplify things for your loved ones should you meet your demise.

At the opening of Jane Austen's novel *Sense and Sensibility*, Mr. Dashwood Sr. has passed away, but on his deathbed he had asked his only son to take care of his stepmother and three stepsisters. The younger Dashwood agrees to do so, but as he is contemplating giving a one-time payment of 3,000 pounds to his step-folk, he and his wife go through a circular discussion where the amount, for various rationales, is reduced to 1,500 pounds, then nothing to the stepsisters but an annuity of 100 pounds a year to his stepmother, then down to giving them a gift of 50 pounds every now and then, and finally to giving them no money at all but assisting them in small ways, such as giving them small presents of fish or game when in season or helping them move out of the house, which he is turning them out of so that his family might live there. In fact, John Dashwood and his wife feel quite put out that his father only considered the feelings of this other side of the family when imploring his son to share some of the 6,000 pounds *a year* that he was to inherit.

While this novel is fiction, there are plenty of real-life examples of the consequences of ignoring estate planning. Read on.

Jennifer and Glenn were partners in a hairstyling business as well as in a common-law relationship. Being a fairly new business, their low reported incomes also made them ineligible for a mortgage with a chartered bank.

When an opportunity arose to buy the building that their business was located in they had to turn to a private investor to secure a mortgage. They didn't have personal life insurance policies on each other, and the private investor naturally didn't have a group mortgage insurance program.

Glenn became sick three years into their business venture and passed away within one month. Jennifer was left grieving for a long period, which impacted her ability to work. Making matters worse, she had to carry the mortgage on her income only, and this was reduced from her taking days off grieving and suffering from depression. After struggling for two years, Jennifer had to close the business.

Grant had a decent job in his earlier years, working in a unionized steel factory with decent pay and benefits. When I spoke to him about insurance needs he told me he was well covered with group insurance coverage of two times his salary. Whether or not this was an appropriate amount mattered not, because Grant did not want me to do a life insurance needs analysis for him.

Unfortunately, Grant was laid off from his job in the mid-nineties, and he spent the next few years looking for work or working in jobs, each with diminishing income levels and benefits. He eventually got work as a security guard on a contract basis with no benefits or group insurance. At this point it was pretty much impossible to get insurance coverage for Grant, because his health had deteriorated. Even if coverage was available to him, it would have been too expensive for him to afford.

Grant was in his early forties when he suffered a massive heart attack. It was an uncomfortable moment in the funeral home when his wife, herself unable to work and on a disability pension, asked me if he had insurance through me.

Robert had been divorced for three years and had lived in another relationship through most of that time. His common-law wife, Linda, had a daughter, Chelsea, from a previous marriage, whom Robert had raised as his own in this short time. He also had three children of his own for which he was still financially responsible.

It was completely unexpected when Robert, aged 54, was found dead on his basement floor apparently from a heart attack thought to be induced from his playing hockey that night.

Robert's will had not been updated since his marriage. Under the old arrangement, his will named his ex-spouse, Mary, as his executor, and she was also to be the beneficiary of his net assets, with his three children named as secondary beneficiaries. Because of his divorce, his ex-spouse was no longer deemed the beneficiary of his assets by law and instead the assets were to be divided among his three children. As part of his divorce agreement he was supposed to have maintained a personal insurance policy with his three children as beneficiaries, but he had let that lapse a year ago when money was tight.

What about Linda and Chelsea? He had insurance coverage through his employer and had designated Linda as the beneficiary, so that went to her, and the home was jointly owned with a right of survivorship, so that passed to Linda as well, without going through his estate. He had also named Linda as the beneficiary of his pension and registered retirement assets. Chelsea was not entitled to anything specifically.

So let's see: he only named his ex-spouse as executor, and that clause gets eliminated, so the courts now have to appoint an executor; his legitimate children have claim only to his personal effects because he held all his valuable assets in ways that weren't included in his estate, and he let the insurance policy where they were named beneficiaries lapse, so they are left with receiving nothing of financial value. His common-law wife of three years receives the greatest financial gain at the expense of his legitimate children, and the lawyers rub their hands together sensing a fight coming on. Do you think this is what Robert had intended to happen?

Ernst and Moira had five children. Ingrid was their only child who did not marry. Being single all her life, Ingrid had made provisions in her will to have her siblings as beneficiaries in a tontine fashion. Her siblings eventually all had children, so she had many nieces and nephews.

By the time Ingrid had passed away at age 88, there was only one sibling, a sister, left alive. All the rest had passed away, as had Ernst and Moira. Because Ingrid had never changed her will upon the births of her nieces and nephews, and all but one of her siblings was gone, her estate of $1.2 million passed on to her sister, who suffered from dementia and also passed away within a few months.

The result: her sister's only child received the entire $1.2 million. Her other nieces and nephews received nothing, including two who had spent many an hour each week caring for her, taking her grocery shopping and to the dentist, and performing other day-to-day activities that were required to maintain her quality of life. Do you think Ingrid anticipated this happening?

These stories are compositions of real events, and they are merely the tip of the iceberg of situations I have seen. I could list even more examples of nightmare estate scenarios, but I think I've made my point that this area is important and requires some thought despite our reluctance to envision our own death.

The process of protecting your loved ones is commonly referred to as estate planning. When we do estate planning what we're really striving for is the smooth transition of your assets to your desired beneficiaries while paying as few taxes as possible after your death. An outline of what an estate plan comprises would include the following:

- Ensuring you have an appropriate amount of life insurance
- Designating a team of professionals
- Drawing up an asset and liability list
- Ensuring you have a will
- Establishing a power of attorney for property
- Establishing a power of attorney for personal care
- Structuring your affairs to minimize taxes and administration fees
- Considering a pre-planned funeral
- Establishing a business succession plan
- Sharing your plans

Life Insurance

While the goal for many people is to eventually be "self-insured," meaning you have so much money that you have no need for insurance, this is often impossible in our younger years. Should we die during our employment years, we need insurance to replace what our working was to accomplish while we were alive. We need to provide income for our families, to provide capital for special needs such as our children's education, and to pay off our debts, such as our mortgage, so our loved ones are not saddled with those burdens after we are gone.

Insurance is a complicated business and life insurance is perhaps the most complicated of them all. While the likelihood of collecting on the other types of insurance is higher than life insurance in any given period, the likelihood of eventually dying is 100 percent. That's why it's best to seek the help of a trusted expert. The problem is that some insurance salespersons can be quite zealous when determining how much insurance you need, and insurance costs money, so that's not a good combination. You need to work with someone whom you trust.

While the main purpose of life insurance is to provide cash to your dependents in order to eliminate any financial burden that may result with your being deceased, it also serves another purpose. It can be thought of as a savings program for the benefit of your heirs.

I will warn you that although life insurance is a necessary pillar of a good financial plan, unfortunately most forms of life insurance, except some group life plans, require some type of medical before you become insurable. Be prepared to spill some blood, in addition to other fluids.

That reminds me of back in my days working at a chartered accounting firm. The firm used to make us students donate blood when we had little to do, and were mostly sitting around in the bull pen. The firm was also very tight in granting raises to its staff. When it came time to do a national survey about how well the firm was treating its employees, I wrote in the comment section that the firm was so cheap that it was selling its staff's blood.

There are two questions that need to be answered: How much life insurance do you need? And what type should you have?

I address the types of life insurance you should consider and how to determine how much insurance you need in Part II of this book—"The Whole Tablecloth." For now, as a rule of thumb, most people are best served by some form of permanent insurance policy—be it a term-to-100 policy, universal life, or whole-life. These policies guarantee protection and a financial legacy for your loved ones for your entire life. At the end, there *will* be something to show for your years of paying premiums. If you can't be bothered determining the amount of insurance you need (it does cost money, after all, so you really should try to put a little effort into calculating it), then as a rule of thumb most people would likely fall somewhere in the $300,000 to $700,000 range.

Designate a Team of Professionals

Make use of smart, knowledgeable, trustworthy professionals—an accountant, a lawyer, and a financial adviser can provide significant guidance. For most people, the passing of a loved one is a time of grief, and the last thing we need is to leave our loved ones burdened with trying to figure out how to handle our estate. The fewer decisions they have to make, the better.

That is why designating a team of professionals is a good idea. Assumedly you are currently dealing with professionals whom you trust, so it makes sense that you should trust them after your death also.

For the sake of your heirs, and even more so your executors, write down the names and contact information of the professionals with whom you deal and let your chosen executor know where you keep the list.

Create an Asset/Liability List

Make life easy for your executors. If you recall, we have already discussed the need to have a household balance sheet in order to monitor the progress of our wealth creation. An asset/liability list is merely a detailed list of the financial institutions and account numbers of where you do business as was summarized on your balance sheet. The list should also show your insurance policies and don't forget information about any safety deposit boxes.

The asset/liability list and the household balance sheet serve to tell your executors what assets and liabilities you have and where they are located, including the gold coins you've got squirreled away in the backyard. Just make sure your treasure map is easy to follow. The list makes things much easier for them when consolidating and distributing your estate. And believe me, it is considered a blessing by any poor executor who has to run around trying to figure out where everything is, particularly for those of you who spread your wealth around rather than consolidating it. Do them a favour by putting your statements in a folder where they can find them.

Your financial coach will likely have a simple workbook that he can give you to fill in. If you don't have access to a workbook, then I find the easiest way to create this list is to just take your last statement received from each institution and put it in a file folder and keep it with your will. Any additional information that you might want to include, like the safety deposit box details, can be written on a piece of paper and included in the folder.

Ensure You Have a Will

So, you don't have a will yet? Have you ever thought about what happens if you die without having one?

This is known as dying intestate, and each province has its own rules as to how your assets are to be divided if you do so. You likely won't appreciate how they want to do it, so it's best to have a will drafted. Common-law or same-sex marriages aren't necessarily recognized either. It depends on the province where you reside, so your common-law partner of 15 years may find herself with none of your assets should you pass away intestate.

Wills and last testaments aren't expensive to have prepared in the overall scheme of things. Some of the things you'll want to ensure your will includes:

- Executors are named, have the ability, and are willing to perform their duties.
- Executors have the freedom to take advantage of tax strategies, investment decisions, etc.
- Executors are allowed access to professional help.
- Guardians are named for minor children.
- Beneficiaries are designated.

I'll admit, some of the above decisions aren't easy ones, and you should make sure your chosen executors and guardians agree to be so before you finalize your will. Just because you name them in your will doesn't mean they have to do it.

What happens to your estate if you die without a will?		
Here's a sample of how various provinces handle intestate estates.		
	Spouse and one child	Spouse and more than one child
Ontario	First $200,000 to spouse; balance split between child and spouse.	First $200,000 to spouse; 1/3 of the balance to spouse; remaining 2/3 divided amongst the children.
British columbia	First $65,000 to spouse (including common-law and same-sex); balance split evenly.	First $65,000 to spouse (including common-law and same-sex); 1/3 of the balance to spouse; remaining 2/3 divided amongst the children.
Alberta	First $40,000 to spouse; balance split between child and spouse.	First $40,000 to spouse; 1/3 of the balance to spouse; remaining 2/3 divided amongst the children.
PEI	Split equally between spouse and child.	1/3 to spouse; 2/3 split amongst children.

Source: CCH Canada Limited, 2011

I think it is a worthwhile exercise to discuss your intentions with your team of professionals so that your will is prepared correctly and so that situations that you may not envision can be brought to light. Review your will periodically and update it for changes that occur throughout your life.

Have Power of Attorney Documents

Along with a will, a *continuing power of attorney for property* and a *power of attorney for personal care* (which can include a "living will" directive specifying treatment you want done if you become ill and can't communicate your wishes) should also be drawn up by a lawyer in case you become incapable of making decisions for yourself regarding your finances or medical treatment while still alive. This will help to ensure that your wishes are carried out even if you're incapacitated for whatever reason. Without one, in Ontario for example, a family member has the right to make your health-care decisions or apply to become your "guardian of property." This alone can create infighting. You should be the one who decides who is going to make decisions if you become incapable.

Minimize Taxes and Administration Costs

When you pass away your will is usually probated. Probate is a judicial certification, basically a blessing by the province's court system that your will is valid and it grants the people you have chosen to administer your will the authority to do so. Why is it needed?

Well, some people have more than one will floating around out there, and it needs to be determined which one represents the deceased's final wishes. Your financial institutions need to know they are giving up your assets to the correct party. If they pay out your assets to your executor and another will is found to be valid with a different executor, then they'll have to pay out again to the second executor and try to recover their money from the first executor. If they pay out to the wrong executor under a probated will, then it's up to the two executors to duke it out on behalf of the estate.

> **Don't be surprised!**
>
> Despite what you may have heard, all investment firms require your will to be probated. They may waive the probate condition if the value of your account is below a set level but this threshold is around $30,000 at most brokerage firms. It doesn't matter that you are the spouse and the sole beneficiary. If your assets are all going to your spouse consider holding them joint-trust-with-right-of-survivorship and designating your spouse as beneficiary on your registered accounts and insurance-based products.

The problem with probate, besides the time involved while the estate is in limbo, is that there is a processing fee applied against the value of your estate in order to probate it. There are other administration costs associated with your estate. Your executors are allowed to charge your estate a fee for the role they play in performing your final wishes. Lawyers will also charge a fee for their role, and this fee is often tied to the value of your estate being probated. The higher the value of your estate, the higher your legal costs might be, and these costs will typically put provincial probate fees to shame. It is the combination of these costs that make the "avoid probate" goal a worthy one on simple estate situations.

There are ways to avoid and reduce probate and administration fees. As examples, you can designate beneficiaries on any insurance-based investments and products (these include insurance policies, guaranteed investment certificates, segregated funds, and variable annuities); you can hold assets and investments in a joint-trust-with-right-of-survivorship manner; you can gift prior to your death; and you can designate beneficiaries on registered accounts, such as RRSPs.

If your spouse is the sole beneficiary of your estate, then most of these techniques are applicable and practical; however, if there are others involved or if your spouse is deceased already, or if you never had a spouse, there may be serious estate distribution consequences when using these techniques. You might also mess up significant income tax saving possibilities if you don't understand all the consequences of what you are doing.

More complicated planning involves establishing inter-vivos trusts (these are trusts set up and funded while you are alive), testamentary trusts (these are established and funded upon your death), and estate freezes to reduce taxes. Make sure you seek advice from a person who understands how the tax system works.

Avoid litigation

Gifts you make prior to your death may be challenged by other beneficiaries if your sanity is questionable (for example, if you are suffering from dementia) or if it is felt that you were under undue influence.

If you put assets into joint tenancy (such as listing a child on a bank account so she can help you do day-to-day banking) and there are other heirs to your estate, the other beneficiaries may claim that the surviving joint owner holds the property in trust for all the beneficiaries, while the surviving joint owner may claim that the right of survivorship applies.

Need an example of how messed up things can get? When I started my career I came across a situation where a woman had made her second husband, James, her executor and the beneficiary of the family home where they resided, which was held in her name only, as well as the remainder of her estate, but she made her son from a previous marriage, Theodore, the beneficiary of her RRIF. What was the result? Her son received an inheritance valued at $300,000, and her husband received a home worth $120,000 (which was really half his anyway) and a tax liability of $138,000 to pay as a result of the taxes on her RRIF. They eventually settled the situation, but only after both participants had sought legal advice and paid for negotiations.

Ways to avoid probate

Your Asset	Own Jointly	Designate Beneficiary	Inter Vivos Trusts	Multiple Wills
Principal residence	✓		✓	
Cottage	✓		✓	
Registered accounts (RRSP, RRIF, LIRA, etc)		✓		
TFSA		✓		
Non-registered accounts (Bank accts, GICs, Brokers)	✓		✓	
Life insurance		✓		
Insurance-based investments (GIAs, segregated funds)	✓	✓		
Private business shares			✓	✓

Source: The Estate Planning Toolkit for Business Owners

This table demonstrates ways that you can avoid probate, but they may have consequences. Talk to your lawyer and adviser so that you understand all the implications of these techniques.

Pre-plan Your Funeral

Pre-planning a funeral is often done by people in order to pre-pay the cost and to a have a say regarding the funeral home arrangements, where they are to be interred, whether they are to be buried or cremated, etc. It works extremely well in reducing the decisions your loved ones have to make in a time of grief. Give this some serious consideration and talk to the funeral home director of your choice to understand what's involved.

Business Succession Planning

If you run your own business, estate planning is extremely important. Life does not just carry on for your business when you are gone. I suggest that you read the book *Every Family's Business* by Thomas William Deans. It will give you an excellent starting point in your thought process.

Share Your Plans!

It doesn't do a whole lot of good if you go about properly structuring your estate matters and then forget to tell someone what you've done. Keep your documents in a safe place and let persons that you trust, such as your chosen executors, know where they may find these documents upon your death.

BAPKIN scratch:

Protect your loved ones at a time when they are feeling much grief. Have permanent life insurance, a will, and powers of attorney; make an asset / liability list; and share your intentions and information with your designated team of professionals who are there to help you and your heirs.

None of us want to think of our own demise, but you really do need to give it a thought and put a little bit of effort into your planning. There are some significant savings that can be achieved from a tax perspective, but make sure you seek trusted professional advice.

I have adequate life insurance coverage: Yes No

I have an updated will: Yes No

I have updated powers of attorney for property and personal care: Yes No

I have made a list of the institutions where all my assets are kept and where I have my debts: Yes No

I have listed the professionals whom I deal with: Yes No

I have considered whether it is practical to try to avoid probate: Yes No

I have shared my intentions: Yes No

Step 6: Understand Tax Matters

Taxes are a very complicated business and have an enormous impact on your wealth. You are encouraged to get professional help, but you should also have a basic understanding of tax minimization strategies in order to understand what your adviser and accountant are doing.

For most individuals, tax planning should be done with the help of a professional. Recognize that computer tax preparation software is a great tool for helping you prepare your tax return, but it doesn't give you tax planning strategies, nor does it ensure that all tax credits or deductions are utilized. It does have its limitations. There are many nuances in tax laws, and they are continually changing, so it is a dangerous thing to try to figure them out on your own.

Understanding the Canadian Tax System

The tax system is one of the most misunderstood areas of finance for people. I can't tell you how many times I've heard people say things that don't make any sense because of their misunderstanding of how taxes are calculated.

Canada has a progressive tax system, meaning that the more income you make, the greater the percent you pay of your income. However, the percent you pay and the calculation of your taxes payable is done in tiers which are called "tax brackets." Tax brackets are ranges of income that are covered under a particular tax rate. For example, in

2011, any income earned between $41,545 and $83,088 is taxed by the federal government at a rate of 22.0 percent. The next federal bracket captures income ranging from $83,089 to $128,800 and is taxed at 26.0 percent, or four percentage points more.

The easiest way to explain the concept of the progressive tax system in action is to show you an example. Let's pretend that the federal income taxes and the provincial income taxes that you pay all have the same brackets. In reality they don't, which leads to a whole bunch of small tax brackets and a more complicated system, but it's the concept of how the calculation works that is important to understand.

Let's say that you earn $85,000, and besides assuming that the federal and provincial tax brackets are the same, let's also assume that the provinces all apply the same tax rate of one half of whatever the federal government charges.

If these assumptions were true, here's what the tax brackets would look like:

First $41,544 of income 22.5% marginal tax	15% federal + 7.5% provincial =
$41,545 to $83,088 33% marginal tax	22% federal + 11% provincial =
$83,089 to $128,800 39% marginal tax	26% federal + 13% provincial =

Since we are pretending that we earn $85,000 in taxable income, our taxes payable would be calculated as follows:

First $41,544 at 22.5% = $9,347.40

The next part is trickier. We made $85,000 and just calculated what we owe on the first $41,544 of it. Now we have to calculate what we owe on the next bracket, which ranges from $41,545 to $83,088. That works out to $41,544 of taxable income (calculated as $83,088 - $41,544), and the tax rate of 33 percent applicable to this bracket

The BAPKIN Plan

means we owe another $13,709.52 in tax. The tax was determined by multiplying the $41,544 of income in the second bracket times the tax rate of 33 percent.

We still have to account for more tax, since we made $85,000 in income and have now only calculated tax on $83,088 of it. We have only $1,912 of income to figure out the tax for that falls in the third bracket. This is determined by subtracting $85,000 from $83,088. Since the tax rate on this amount of income is 39 percent, we would owe another $745.68 in tax, calculated by multiplying $1,912 by 39 percent.

Here's a summary of what we calculated:			
First bracket: income of	$41,544	Taxes owing of	$9,347.40
Second bracket: income of	41,544	Taxes owing of	13,709.52
Third bracket: income of	1,912	Taxes owing of	745.68
Total income accounted for	$85,000	Total taxes payable	$ 23,802.60

Now that you have an idea of how a progressive tax system works, let's understand two more concepts that are important—marginal tax rates and average tax rates.

The average tax rate that you pay under this scenario is 28 percent, which is calculated by dividing the total taxes payable of $23,802.60 by your taxable income of $85,000. This is your real total tax rate and is a far cry from the 50 percent that many middle-class people think they pay in taxes.

The confusion lies in what is known as your marginal tax rate. That represents the rate applicable to the bracket that you currently fall into. In the example above, you have a marginal tax rate of 39 percent, because you are in the third tax bracket. If your employer said to you that she would pay you another $1,000 this year, the tax payable on that incremental amount would be 39 percent, because that's the tax bracket that new income would fall into. If you didn't receive the raise and contributed $5,000 to an RRSP, you would get a 39 percent deduction on $1,912 of the contribution and only 33 percent on the remaining $3,088 of the contribution, since the deduction knocks your income back down into the second bracket.

Tax Strategies

Now that we have an understanding of how a progressive tax system works and an understanding of average and marginal tax rates, it's time to explore what we can do to legally minimize our tax burden. The core philosophy in tax planning is determining ways to defer, deduct, divide, and convert income, and to maximize your tax credits and avoid clawbacks. These are what I like to call my grade-six report card (3Ds and 3Cs). What do I mean by all this?

Defer

Let's start with deferrals. We want to defer claiming income that would otherwise be taxed now until a later point in time. The old "put off paying today what you can pay tomorrow." The idea is to claim the income at a later point in time to take advantage of the time value of money and to try to claim it when we are in a lower tax bracket.

How do we do that? The most popular means is to contribute to your company pension plan or a Registered Retirement Savings Plan (RRSP). You must have "earned income" to contribute to an RRSP. Earned income is basically employment income (it doesn't matter whether you're an employee or self-employed) but also includes rental income, taxable support payments, and some other income items. The Notice of Assessment that you receive from the Canada Revenue Agency when you file your tax return each year will let you know the most that you can contribute that year.

RRSP contributions are deferrals because you are eventually taxed on the income when you withdraw it from the registered account. Hopefully you're withdrawing from your registered account when you are retired and in a lower tax bracket and will thus pay less tax than the refund you received when you contributed the money. The income it earns is also sheltered from tax until you withdraw it so that serves as a deferral also.

> **Registered versus non-registered accounts**
>
> A registered retirement account is an investment account whose income is not subject to income tax when it is earned but rather when it is withdrawn from the account. Examples of registered accounts include Registered Retirement Savings Plans (RRSP) and Registered Retirement Income Funds (RRIF).
>
> Some registered accounts have rules regarding how much can be withdrawn from them and when the funds can be withdrawn. These registered accounts are known as Locked-in Retirement Accounts, Locked-in Retirement Income Funds, and Life Income Funds, and they come about if you commute your company pension plan.
>
> Non-registered accounts are investment accounts that don't have any special tax deferral rules or investment restrictions attributable to them. The income earned in these accounts is subject to tax each year and is taxed differently if it comes in the form of interest, dividends, or capital gains. Expenses that are incurred in non-registered accounts are usually deductible.
>
> Expenses that are incurred in registered accounts are not directly tax-deductible on your tax return. It's not all bad however because the expenses are not taxed as having been first withdrawn as income, so in effect, it serves as if you are getting an "embedded" deduction on them.

Another example of means of deferring income is by making use of Corporate Class and T-Class mutual funds. These types of funds allow capital gains to be tax deferred until later points in time.

Deduct

Deductions are write-offs that you are allowed to claim in order to reduce your taxable income. Deductions are most advantageous because you receive a tax benefit at your marginal tax rate, which is *your* highest personal tax rate. This tax savings rate can be as high as almost 50 percent, so don't miss out on any deductions.

Examples of allowable write-offs include

- Annual union or professional fees
- Childcare expenses
- Spousal support payments, made in conjunction with a separation agreement or a court order
- Investment counsel and management fees charged on non-registered accounts
- Safety deposit box fees if you earn investment income in non-registered accounts
- Interest expense that you pay in order to earn taxable investment income such as dividends, interest, and rental income. This does not include interest paid to earn capital gain income
- Accrued interest that you must pay when you buy a bond on the open market
- Moving expenses
- Allowable employment expenses

Many of these deductions have special rules as to when they apply or who can claim them. That's why it's worth your while to have a person who understands tax laws advise you. For example, moving expenses can only be applied against income from a new location, and the taxpayer must move at least 40 kilometres closer to the employer. Heck, even the rules as to how to measure the 40 kilometres are complicated.

> 👍 **THUMBPRINT**
> Investment management/counseling fees that are incurred in order to earn investment income in non-registered accounts can be deducted on your tax return in the year they are incurred.

> 👍 **THUMBPRINT**
>
> If you buy a bond on the open market in your non-registered account and you pay an accrued interest amount, do not forget to deduct this interest on your tax return.

If you make use of an investment counsellor or portfolio manager to manage your non-registered portfolio on a discretionary basis, you are able to deduct these fees against *any income*, which can be a significant tax advantage. Consolidating registered and non-registered accounts with one counsellor can often minimize these fees on an after-tax basis depending on the counsellor. As well, if you buy a bond in the secondary market, which is where most people buy federal government, provincial, and corporate bonds, you will have to pay the interest that has accrued up to your settlement date to the former bondholder. This interest is deductible but many taxpayers miss deducting this expense because there is no fancy tax slip issued to give to the accountant.

Divide

Dividing income includes doing things such as income splitting with spouses and children, pension splitting, and providing spousal investment loans. The purpose of dividing income is to move income from a family member in a high tax bracket to a family member in a lower tax bracket so that lower taxes are paid overall and the family keeps more for themselves. These savings can be substantial often in the range of 20 to 40 percent.

Splitting income with your spouse or children can come in many forms. If you are a self-employed person you can hire your spouse to do bookkeeping or managerial services. Your children can be hired to clean your office, put together mail outs, or whatever jobs may be available that are within their skill set. Then, let them pay for their own hockey equipment or dance lessons. Of course the amount that you pay them must be reasonable.

If you're not self-employed there are still other ways to split income with your spouse. One method is through a spousal investment loan.

With this strategy, you would loan a substantial amount of money to your spouse in order for him to make income producing investments. You need to have a proper demand loan drafted and signed. You can't just hand over the money. You must charge an interest rate on the money you have lent and the minimum rate that can be charged is prescribed by the tax authorities. Though the prescribed rate changes quarterly, your spouse need only pay the rate that was in effect when the loan was granted and this rate can be quite low. For example, the prescribed rate in the winter of 2012 was only 1 percent. That's right—only 1 percent. As long as your spouse pays you this interest each year, within 30 days of the year end, the loan remains legitimate. Of course, your spouse can deduct this interest as an interest expense, but you have to claim it as interest income.

What would happen if you just gifted the money to your spouse? Any investment income earned would not be taxed in his hands but rather in your own. This is what is known as an attribution rule. You may have gotten away with putting money into your spouse's investment account and having him claim the investment income reported on the tax slips in the past, but if Canada Revenue catches up to you, you should recognize that you've committed a no-no. I've known couples who have done this and have been oblivious to having done anything wrong until CanRev came knocking.

If you are retired you are now able to split pension income with your spouse. Your Canada Pension Plans can be split, but you must both follow the same rules and both split with each other. You can't just have one person splitting the CPP and not the other. This splitting is done at the source so you actually receive the adjusted amount.

You are also able to split any formal pension income that you receive from employment or from a RRIF or annuity when you prepare your tax return. In the case of the RRIF or annuity, you must be 65 years of age before you can split this income (it doesn't matter what age your spouse is), whereas the pension from your employment can be split at any time after you are retired. Not fair for those of us who don't have defined-benefit pension plans, I know, but that's life. There's some significant tax savings that can be had by splitting pensions, but you're best having tax software that can calculate it for you because the calculation can be circular and impacts tax credits.

> **Spousal RRSPs still matter**
>
> With the advent of pension splitting, many people no longer are making use of spousal RRSPs, but they still do have their uses.
>
> - If you are older than your spouse and still earn employment income after age 71, you can't contribute to your own RRSP, but you can still make spousal RRSP contributions and get the tax deduction.
> - If you retire before age 65, you can withdraw from your own RRSP and your spouse can withdraw from the spousal RRSP (provided you haven't contributed to a spousal RRSP within three years), thereby creating a "splitting" effect.
> - Contributions can't be made to your own RRSP after the date of your death, but contributions to a spousal RRSP in the year you pass away can be made by your legal representative.

Convert

Some investment products exist that allow you to convert "inefficient" incomes, which are those subject to higher tax rates such as interest income, into "tax-efficient" incomes, such as capital gains, which are subject to lower tax rates. In the scheme of things in Canada, capital gains and dividends are taxed at significantly lower levels than interest and employment incomes, so there can be big tax savings if conversion of income types can be done.

One example of an investment product that lets you convert income is flow-through shares. These shares let you write off your investment as a tax deduction, and then when you sell them or they convert to a mutual fund, any proceeds you receive becomes a capital gain and are therefore subjected to a lower tax rate than the tax deduction you received. While this sounds like a great situation, there are risks involved, since the underlying investments represent shares of exploratory resource companies that are issued at a premium.

You should not invest in flow-through shares without getting proper advice from a qualified financial adviser. Ask your adviser for both the pros and the cons of such an investment relative to your own situation.

Credits

In Canada, the tax system works via deductions and credits. Some tax credits are refundable and some are non-refundable. Refundable credits are amounts that are paid to you in cold hard cash—you get them in the form of reduced taxes payable or a tax refund when you file your tax return. The most common of the refundable credits are the provincial credits that some people get for property taxes, sales taxes, and political contributions.

Most credits are non-refundable credits. That means that if our non-refundable tax credits exceed our taxes payable, we don't get the difference paid to us as a refund.

We want to maximize tax credits as much as possible. There are some tricks involved such as combining medical expense claims and donations. Tax credits are not as beneficial as tax deductions to most taxpayers because credits give you a benefit at the lowest tax rate whereas deductions can give you benefits at higher tax rates.

> Tax credits aren't as beneficial as tax deductions. Most tax credits give you a benefit at the lowest tax rate, whereas tax deductions give you a benefit at your marginal tax rate.

Examples of tax credits that you may be eligible for based on your life situation include

- Basic personal amount
- Age credit
- Married credit or eligible dependant credit
- Disability amount
- Home buyers amount
- Tuition, education, and textbook credit (based on time in school)

Examples of tax credits that arise from your actually having to pay out expenses include

- Tuition, education, and textbook credit (based on tuition fees paid)
- Canada Pension Plan and Unemployment Insurance premiums
- Medical expenses
- Charitable donations

Some credits can also be split or transferred to spouses or persons who support dependents.

Clawbacks

There are other complicated issues in Canadian tax law such as clawbacks on the age credit, Old Age Security, and GST/HST credits, and those clawbacks can add up to big dollars. For example, in Canada you begin to collect Old Age Security (OAS) at age 65. The OAS starts having to be repaid—hence the term "clawback"—if you earn about $67,000 or more, and you'll have to repay the whole amount if you earn more than about $109,000. Old Age Security amounts to more than $6,000 per year and is increased each quarter for inflation, so this is usually something you'd like to keep.

Some people view the Old Age Security clawback as a punitive tax on seniors who may have sacrificed more when younger, while others view it as a social program that's only supposed to help seniors with lower income. Regardless of your perspective, most people would agree that they would sooner be able to keep the money rather than repay it once they receive it.

If you do have to repay any of your Old Age Security payment, you should be aware that you will receive that much less in payments the very next year. If your income level the next year proves to be lower, they will make it up to you by paying you the amount you should have received when you file your tax return. It will come in the form of a refundable tax credit, so make sure you file that tax return on time.

The type of income that you earn in retirement can have a positive or negative impact on your Old Age Security. Only one half of capital gains are reported as income on your tax return, so this will have an effect of helping you keep your OAS. Dividends on the other hand, while taxed at a lower rate, are first grossed up and included in your income. This gross up has a negative effect on your refundable credit calculations and OAS clawback.

What does all this mean? It means get professional help in tax planning and tax preparation and in retirement income solutions. There are just too many pitfalls and opportunities that can be messed up. Make sure your financial adviser has a strong understanding of Canadian taxes as well as investment characteristics. Can't tell? It certainly would help if your adviser had an accounting or financial planning designation behind his or her name. Be sure to give your permission for your professionals to work together.

Not all incomes are taxed equal

Here's an example of how different investment returns are taxed in Canada

* marginal tax rates based on a taxable income of $75,000 in 2011.

	Interest income	Capital gains	Eligible dividends
Ontario	32.98%	16.49%	12.50%
British Columbia	32.50%	16.25%	8.11%
Alberta	32.00%	16.00%	7.85%
PEI	38.70%	19.35%	16.59%

Source: Ernst & Young

BAPKIN scratch:

Reduce your taxes by understanding and making use of the 3 Cs (convert, credits, clawbacks) and 3 Ds (defer, deduct, divide). Use a qualified professional to advise you about your tax situation.

Don't be penny wise and pound foolish. The cost of professional advice is minimal when compared to the substantial tax savings that can be had.

We are always trying to reduce the amount of taxes that we pay. That's because, for most people, this is one of the most significant expenses that we incur. Whenever possible, you should be looking at ways to defer, deduct, and divide (split) your income. There are also ways to convert income to more tax-friendly, lower rates. Maximizing tax credits is a legitimate way to reduce taxes and planning must be done to ensure you are not subject to clawbacks.

I understand how a progressive tax system works: Yes No

I understand the difference between an average tax and a marginal tax rate: Yes No

I understand the difference between a tax deduction and a tax credit: Yes No

I have sought out professional tax advice and preparation: Yes No

Step 7: Have a Personal Pension Plan Strategy

If you're a pre-boomer, you've lived in an era where almost 50 percent of workers had pension plans of a "guaranteed" nature. Fast forward to today and it's estimated that fewer than 20 percent of non-public sector workers have such plans. Chances are, if you are a late-boomer or younger, you have to provide for your own retirement, including making the investment decisions and making up for any deficiency in your investment returns. Welcome back to the nineteenth century.

These are tough times, although the way people have spent and structured their lives, you'd never know it. Life seems pretty good. We've gone through a period of sustained high employment; many families have two incomes, which provide plenty of cash flow, and interest rates are low, which have made mortgage payments cheap and house prices appreciate.

But there is a Mr. Hyde aspect to the times we live in. Because interest rates are low, guaranteed investment returns, including investments such as annuities and GICs, are low also. This makes it very difficult to provide income in retirement and have our investments grow. As well, world stock markets have had negative returns for a decade. What's the impact? Many people's savings have barely grown in the past decade, which puts even further pressure and stress on our retirement plans.

The BAPKIN Plan

There are typically four major life stages that we go through in retirement planning: the accumulation stage, the acceleration stage (when we are about 5 to 10 years from our planned retirement), the retirement stage, and the distribution stage (where we start thinking, like Fred Sanford, that "the big one" may be coming).

The BAPKIN recommendation is that you understand what stage you are in and to decide and follow a strategy relevant to that stage. So let's look at what each stage entails. You will get much more out of the chapter if you concentrate on the stage or stages that are relevant to you now or in the near future and skim over or ignore the stages that aren't.

Accumulation Stage

The accumulation stage is the growth stage, which takes place through most of your working years up until about 10 years before your planned retirement. At this stage your main concerns are sticking to a savings program and how you invest these savings. There is usually quite some time before you are entering into retirement, so your risk tolerance for your investments is usually higher than in your later years.

> 👍 **THUMBPRINT**
>
> **TFSA or RRSP?**
>
> BOTH if you can do it, but if not the decision gets tougher. If you think you'll be in a lower tax bracket when you take out the money than when you put it in, then the RRSP gets the nod, but if you are likely going to be in the same or a higher tax bracket (perhaps because of an inheritance?), then the TFSA wins out. "Getting a refund" is not a legitimate reason for the RRSP to get the nod over the TFSA, however, since the refund is merely the present value of your future tax payment. For most middle-class people, the TFSA may get a slight nod provided the money is left for retirement purposes, because it helps preserve the tax credits available to seniors.

We have already discussed the need to save 10 to 15 percent of your take-home pay and the need to track your wealth in order to reinforce your desire to save. How should you be investing these savings? For most Canadians, it makes sense to invest within both a Registered Retirement Savings Plan (RRSP) and a Tax-Free Savings Account (TFSA).

Suggested Strategies for the Accumulation Stage

Build an investment pyramid. An investment pyramid is most appropriate for investors who are conservative and just learning about investments. It entails investing your savings first into conservative, guaranteed investments, such as GICs and bonds, and then as your wealth builds, to slowly divert savings to more growth-oriented investments, such as balanced and equity mutual funds and individual stocks or professionally managed portfolios.

This strategy is good for novice investors because it lets them learn about investments and lets them get a feel for what risk and volatility they can handle in a real-world setting. The negative aspect of this strategy is that you lose valuable time that would be available for faster compounding in growth-oriented investments.

Conversely, some advisers believe that it's best for young people to go 100 percent directly into equity mutual funds instead, since you have a long time for your investments to recover from any market setbacks and your initial savings represent a small portion of your lifetime savings anyway. It also lets you develop an "emotional" tolerance for risk while the stakes are low. As your savings grow, you would then build out an "inverse pyramid," allocating savings to more conservative investments as you get older.

Personal pension plan portfolio. This strategy is ideal for people who need or want to see a "guaranteed" growth in their portfolios. (Fine print: absolutely nothing is truly guaranteed in the investment world, even if it has the word "guaranteed" in it, but this strategy is about the closest thing you're going to get to it with minimum costs and better growth potential.)

In effect, this strategy works like a minimum return pension plan. It involves investing a substantial portion of your savings in long-term government strip bonds (these are compound bonds) that will coincide with your likely or targeted retirement date, and the remaining savings are allocated to a growth investment. When I adopt this approach for clients I generate two return targets: a "minimum target" and a "possible/probable target."

For example, a new client, Gwen, came to see me a few years ago. She was 45 years of age and had $100,000 in her RRSP that she was looking at investing. Gwen planned on retiring in 20 years' time and was nervous about the markets. She just wanted to be assured that there would be some growth for planning purposes, regardless of how small it might be. After all, she didn't want to be like her cousin Fred, who invested all his money in global equity funds at the start of the millennium and who was still down 30 percent after a decade. She wanted more certainty.

When Gwen came to see me, five-year GIC rates were around 2.5 percent, and a 20-year Province of Ontario strip bond was yielding about 4.35 percent. If Gwen would be happy with seeing her capital grow comparable to the 2.5 percent GIC for the 20-year period, then she would expect to see her capital grow to $164,000. This is her minimum target.

In order to satisfy Gwen's objective, I could allocate $70,000 of her capital to the 20-year strip bond at 4.35 percent. This investment would be worth $164,000 when it matured in 20 years. The remaining $30,000 of her capital could be allocated to an equity investment, such as a mutual fund. If the mutual fund investment collapsed to absolutely nothing (unlikely if you are properly diversified) then Gwen would see her capital grow to $164,000 (i.e., the 2.5 percent rate of return that she wanted to earn as a minimum). If the mutual fund did not earn a penny throughout the 20 years, then Gwen's portfolio would be worth $194,000.

But if the mutual fund grew at 8 percent, which would be more in line with historical returns, then it would be worth $140,000, and her total portfolio would be worth $304,000, a return of 5.72 percent or more than twice what five-year GICs were earning at the time. This was her possible/probable target.

In times like we have been experiencing where investors have seen no growth and even negative growth in their portfolios, this strategy satisfies the investors' behavioural demons. It lets them participate in the stock markets that have greater growth potential, and it lets them focus on the longer term knowing that their portfolio will grow regardless of what is happening in the markets.

Balanced portfolio/growth portfolio. For most investors who have some experience with the capital markets, a balanced portfolio or a growth portfolio, depending on your risk tolerance, is likely the most appropriate strategy to employ while in your accumulation stage.

A balanced portfolio will typically have an asset mix consisting of cash, fixed income, and equity investments. A growth portfolio is similar to a balanced portfolio, except there is a greater weighting toward equity investments.

While there are no guarantees, such portfolios typically will outperform the other strategies listed previously over 10- and 20-year time frames. For example, the median 20-year return on a Canadian balanced mutual fund is about 7.0 percent to the end of December 2010. An investor who invested $100,000 in the median fund 20 years ago would now have a portfolio worth approximately $394,000. If you had been more aggressive and invested in a portfolio equally weighted between the average Canadian equity and global equity balanced mutual funds, your return would have approximated 6.4 percent ($305,000). These returns incorporate two very significant bear makers in the past 10 years and compare favourably to the five-year GIC average index of 4.7 percent over the same time frame ($253,000).

For most persons in the accumulation stage, I believe that a balanced portfolio is the most appropriate approach providing they can handle the volatility that comes with it. If not, then go with my patent-pending "personal pension plan" approach and sleep at night.

> **The Individual Pension Plan (IPP)**
>
> If you are a business owner or an executive older than 40 years of age and earning more than $128,000 per year, your employer (which may be you) may be eligible to establish a registered defined-benefit pension for you. These plans are an effective means of saving for retirement but do come at a cost. For more information on IPPs see Part II, "The Whole Tablecloth."

Acceleration Stage

The acceleration stage is the period in your life where you start giving serious thought to retirement. For many people, this is where they also get serious about socking money away for retirement, and their risk tolerances vary widely. Some investors become more aggressive, hoping that their investments will help make up for the shortfall in their savings discipline for the last 30 years, while others become more conservative, fearing that there isn't much more time to put money away or make up for losses.

From a savings perspective, this should be a time when your mortgage is paid off and the kids are almost done university. If you've got the spare cash flow, this is the time you sock away more of your leftover money. If you don't have much extra, you had better review how extravagant your lifestyle is and start contemplating the need to work longer.

Suggested Strategies for the Acceleration Stage

Personal pension plan portfolio. Previously discussed in the Accumulation phase, this approach makes sense to continue if this has been your strategy since that time.

If you adopt this strategy this close to your planned retirement, the result will be a very high emphasis on fixed income investments, somewhere in the ballpark of 90 percent or more. That's not necessarily a bad thing, but you may feel so if the stock markets prove to have a great decade of 15-plus percent returns (it's been done before) and you're sitting there making less than 4 percent.

Still, if you're conservative, have saved a significant portion of your required capital, and have a reasonable and supportable lifestyle, this approach does have its merits.

Balanced portfolio. At this stage, most people should be getting more conservative with their investments and should be adjusting their asset mix so that a greater emphasis is on guaranteed returns; however, it will likely not be to the extent that a Personal Pension Plan portfolio would have you do. An income with growth emphasis would be appropriate for most investors who have an average level of risk tolerance. Over the past 20 years, such a portfolio averaged about 7 percent thanks to the high interest rates that existed in the early 1990s. The 10-year performance is a more modest 3 percent, because interest rates have been significantly lower.

> **👍 THUMBPRINT**
>
> When determining a starting point for how much you should have in equities and fixed income, use your age plus 5 to 10 years as an approximation of how much you should have in fixed income investments if you are a conservative investor in the Acceleration stage. Therefore, if you're 55 years of age, it will likely be appropriate to have 60 to 65 percent of your portfolio in bonds or GICs and 35 to 40 percent in growth-oriented investments, such as stocks or equity mutual funds.

Some investors can afford to be more aggressive and have a heavier weighting in equity investments if they have significant market experience, a guaranteed income source at retirement, or perhaps expect to receive a sizeable inheritance. The thumbprint is a conservative guideline only.

Segregated mutual funds portfolio. If you want to have a more aggressive asset mix but you still want some protection for your portfolio, a segregated fund will provide a capital guarantee if you hold the investment for 10 years or more. A few years ago we would have scoffed at such a guarantee as being pretty much useless, but the past 10 years have proven that a loss, though rare, is possible over a 10-year period.

Even if you are making use of segregated mutual funds, the insurance companies no longer guarantee a full 100 percent of your capital as they did in the 1990s (it's now usually only 75 percent), so it is prudent to have some fixed income investments in these portfolios so that you likely won't suffer the 25 percent loss in the long-term.

> **Understanding Segregation**
>
> Don't get confused by the term "segregated" on your brokerage statements. Segregated mutual funds are insurance company products that have various bells and whistles attached to them. But if you look at your brokerage statement you may see that your non-insurance investments are held in "segregated" form. This simply means that the securities you own are held in trust and are segregated from the assets of the brokerage firm for your protection.

Variable annuity portfolio. A variable annuity provides you with an income guarantee for life, and if there is some of your capital left when you die, the capital goes to your beneficiaries. But you don't need the income at this time of your life, so why is it a potential strategy at this stage? The reason lies in the feature that provides a bonus return for every year that you don't take any income from the portfolio. If you know that you are going to put some of your savings into a variable annuity when you are at the retirement stage, it may be worth your while to put the capital into such an investment before that time to collect the bonus.

The balanced portfolio is the typical strategy that investors follow at the accumulation stage, but the variable annuity strategy is gaining popularity among conservative investors, who know they are going to want guaranteed income.

Retirement Stage

At this stage you leave the work force, either on a full-time or part-time basis, and start enjoying the fruits of your years of labour. Your savings program usually stops now and instead you start depleting your capital and living off any income that it might generate. Investors are typically more conservative at this time of their lives because they feel they cannot replace any significant capital losses.

If you find that you haven't saved enough, the answer is not to get more risky in your investment approach. Instead, consider working past your planned retirement date or working part time. A part-time job is sometimes all that it takes for a plan to come together and many people have the opportunity to offer their services to their former employers on a consulting basis. It's a lot easier going to work when you know that you only have to do it for two or three days a week and it can possibly provide some very important side-benefits, such as providing a social network and a reason for getting up in the morning.

No one strategy has to stand on its own. Depending on the amount of savings you have, you can mix and match them according to your needs and objectives.

Suggested Strategies for the Retirement Stage

Pension Plan approach. Why not treat your retirement savings as if you were in a defined-benefit plan? How do you do this? Well, when it comes time that you need to draw income, allocate your registered savings to a life annuity just as your employer may have done. You can even invest in annuities with inflation protection and those that will continue paying to your spouse when you die (but at lower initial income amounts, of course) just like a defined-benefit pension would do. This approach is great for those who want or need to maximize income and aren't concerned that this money will no longer be available as an estate for their heirs.

Of course, you might find that once you have saved and scrimped through your working years, it can be quite hard to hand over all your savings to an insurance company, never to be able to access them again, in return for a promise of guaranteed income to be provided for the remainder of your life. There is a psychological barrier for many people to go solely with this alternative, since we hate losing control and access to our capital and many feel, rightly or wrongly, that their estate is getting ripped off when no capital is returned upon death.

Guarantee your living expenses (product allocation). This strategy involves allocating a portion of your retirement savings to life annuities and variable annuities to ensure that your essential lifestyle expenses will be covered for your entire life. You'll be able to sleep at night knowing that this income will be paid to you monthly regardless of where interest rates are going or how the market is doing. Annuities can be good investments for people with very limited investment experience.

The amount that you would need to allocate to an annuity or a variable annuity depends on what you are receiving from the other guaranteed pensions you are entitled to (e.g., your Canada Pension [or Quebec], Old Age Security, and your company pension). Any leftover savings that you might have can be allocated to more traditional investments such as GICs, bonds, and mutual funds to provide additional income so that you can then satisfy your lifestyle expenses and estate concerns.

If you are investing a significant amount into annuities, it makes sense to use more than one annuity provider in order to take advantage of the insurance that is offered to protect your payment similar to the insurance that banks have for their GICs. Annuities in Canada are insured up to $2,000 per month, or 85 percent of the payment if over $2,000, so if you were investing $500,000 in an annuity, your adviser might recommend that you spread it amongst several different providers. Annuity payments also depend on where interest rates are when you first invest in the annuity, so if you're unsure whether long-term interest rates are going to rise or fall, you may want to invest in stages rather than putting everything into one annuity all at once.

A variable annuity is a hybrid investment that gives you the guaranteed-income-for-life feature of an annuity but also lets you access your capital, should you need it, and your heirs will get any amount of capital that is remaining after your death. Sounds great, but it will pay you less each month than a life annuity does, and there won't necessarily be anything left after 20 years thanks to the higher fees involved (basically an insurance cost) and depending on your investment success.

In its most pure form, the product allocation philosophy allocates your capital between life annuities, variable annuities, and tax-class mutual funds, but really, the core point is to use some form of annuity to guarantee your basic living expenses for life and then invest the rest of your savings in a manner that will let you sleep at night, minimize taxes, provide income, and satisfy your financial legacy and as many lifestyle objectives as possible.

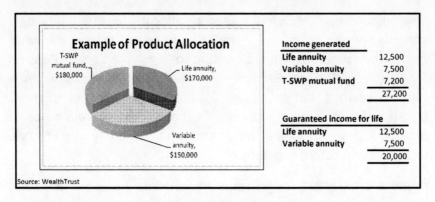

Figure 7-1 *Product allocation provides guaranteed income levels with some access to your capital, some tax efficiency, and some potential for having an estate for your heirs.*

The BAPKIN Plan

Product Allocation:

Product:	What does it protect against?			What can it possibly do for us?		
	Negative returns	Inflation	Living a long life	Provide liquidity	Provide growth	Provide an estate
CPP and OAS	✓	✓	✓	✗	✗	✗ [1]
Employment pension	✓	✗✓ [2]	✓	✗	✗	✗
Life annuities	✓	✗✓ [3]	✓	✗	✗	✗
Variable annuities	✓	✓ [4]	✓	✓ [5]	✓ [6]	✓ [7]
T-SWP mutual fund	✗	✓ [4]	✗	✓	✓	✓

1- the CPP provides a very small death benefit.
2- not all pensions are indexed for inflation. Some are not at all and others may only partially be indexed.
3- annuities are not indexed for inflation unless you specifically invest in an indexed annuity.
4- variable annuities and T-SWP mutual funds only protect you from inflation if the markets you are invested in provide returns better than inflation.
5- variable annuities give you access to your capital but at the expense of affecting your guaranteed withdrawal amount. They are not as liquid as T-SWPs.
6- variable annuity investments have higher fees than comparable T-SWP mutual funds so though they can provide growth, they will be less effective than a T-SWP.
7- variable annuity investments only provide an estate if you die before your capital pool runs out of money. Since you are drawing on your capital first before the insurance company is obligated to pay you any of its capital, there may be nothing left for an estate should you live long and have poor investment returns.

Source: *Pensionize Your Nest Egg*

Traditional investing with a cash wedge. Some people don't like the idea of annuities because the capital is usually surrendered to the insurance company when the investor dies. I'll note here that you can invest in annuities that guarantee a number of years of payments, but it comes at a price—namely, a lower monthly annuity payment throughout your life, and once the minimum payment period is over, your remaining capital still gets surrendered to the insurance company. Instead of having their capital surrendered, some investors would prefer to continue to invest in a traditional portfolio with investments like GICs, bonds, stocks, and mutual funds.

Indeed, if you have enough capital saved which will provide income to cover your various expenses, and particularly if you have investment experience, you might be quite happy not making use of annuities and potentially leaving a greater estate value.

> 👍 **THUMBPRINT**
>
> Oh NO! The market has undergone a correction and you need to take money out of your portfolio. Don't sweat it; just get a little more frugal. If you were planning on taking 4 percent or more out of your portfolio after enduring a significant correction, don't do it. A withdrawal rate of 3 percent goes a long way to preserving capital!

An investor using the traditional portfolio strategy in the retirement stage is likely best served with a portfolio that emphasizes mostly income-oriented investments but with some growth. By taking out a maximum 3 or 4 percent to live on, your capital can last a long time and very likely more than a life time.

Investments, particularly those that are associated with the stock market, have seen a significant amount of volatility in the last 15 years, and we may find the same thing happening with long-term bonds at some time in the future. We want to make sure that we don't get spooked out of our investments at times when volatility reigns, and one way to do that is to have a cash reserve, which we call a "cash wedge," that is available to pay out our cash needs over the next three years and which will give our longer-term investments time to recover from any setbacks that may occur.

> 👍 **THUMBPRINT**
>
> If you don't have a company pension or other guaranteed income sources at retirement, you should have approximately 60 to 75 percent of your portfolio in fixed income investments, such as bonds or GICs, and about 25 to 40 percent in growth-oriented investments, such as stocks or equity mutual funds.

In the example per Figure 7-2, I'm showing a cash wedge that ladders the cash flow we will be taking out of the account over the next three years. The cash wedge is comprised of the daily interest savings account (for the current year's withdrawal), a one-year GIC for next year's withdrawal, and a two-year GIC for the year after. If the markets correct, we will not have to draw income from the longer-term mutual fund investments for the next three years. We can sell parts of the mutual fund investments when conditions are more favourable in order to replenish our cash wedge, or we can make use of mutual funds that pay out a set percentage each month so we don't have to worry about market timing.

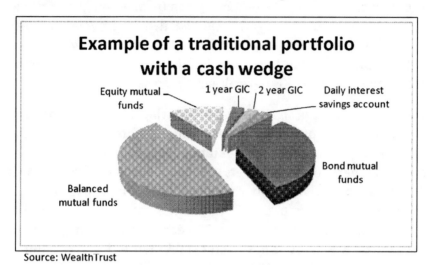

Source: WealthTrust

Figure 7-2 *This illustration demonstrates a traditional portfolio consisting of bonds and stocks held through mutual funds with a cash wedge component to provide retirement income over the next three years.*

Traditional investing with buckets. "Buckets" is a term we use when we talk about having different pools of capital meant for different purposes. We can have separate accounts established for goals such as passing on inheritances, investing for income, and investing for growth.

If used properly, separate accounts can let us set different investment objectives with different risk tolerances and time horizons; this can contribute to better performance overall, because it may help us to stay invested with the proper focus. For example, if you know you want to buy a new car in three years, you can open a separate account and transfer the money into that account that will pay for the car and invest it in a manner consistent with such a short-term objective. You may also have a goal of providing an estate of at least $200,000 for your heirs. If you have an adequate amount of capital, you can set aside this amount in a separate account and either invest it conservatively and live off the income it generates or you can invest it in a longer-term investment perhaps with some capital protection mechanism or with better estate efficiency.

The monies that you have remaining can be invested in a portfolio with a medium or longer-term perspective to provide you with income and tax efficiency. You will be less afraid to deplete some of the capital from this third pool, if necessary, since you know the estate and vehicle needs have already been set aside.

There's a psychological advantage to knowing that money has been put aside in an appropriate investment in another area. Like the cash wedge, the bucket allows you to be less panicky when market conditions deteriorate and it lets you see more clearly when making decisions appropriate to your various financial objectives and risk tolerances. For example, you may feel a lot more comfortable depleting your RRIF to nil over a 30-year time frame if you know that a separate account has been established to transfer another part of your wealth to your heirs, on a tax-efficient basis.

Layered income approach. The *layered income* approach is a tax-focussed method of meeting your income requirements by using different income sources and investment products that have different types of tax treatment. The idea is to use regularly taxed income sources at your lower tax brackets and then use your capital to make use of more tax-efficient income sources to supplement your income needs. If done correctly, layering should minimize clawbacks and the amount of tax you pay on the income you receive while maximizing tax credits.

Sound complicated? That's because it is. It requires having a strong understanding of tax and investment products and the capability to provide any of the products that you need. It can be very effective at minimizing taxes, because our tax system is progressive rather than flat, meaning income tax rates rise up on a graduated or marginal basis. In order for your adviser to do this strategy properly, you should consolidate your assets with him so he can see the total income effects of the various investments that you are employing and make annual adjustments accordingly. Just be sure that your adviser truly understands what he is doing both in the tax and investment realms.

Your "personal" pension plan approach. At the retirement stage, your frame of mind should be that you are creating for yourself a "personal" pension plan. You and your adviser should be creating a unique approach that embodies the above mentioned strategies. You need to prioritize what is most important to you: an estate for the kids, maximizing income, minimizing taxes, sleeping at night knowing that you won't be destitute—whatever.

Once you know the objectives that you have for this stage of your life, choose your strategies so that the most important objectives are met. Recognize that there is always going to be good and bad with each strategy just as there is good and bad with the key investment products that you're likely to utilize at this stage.

Other considerations. There are some important key considerations that you should give thought to when deciding what strategy you should implement for your retirement savings. They include your expected sources of income, any estate concerns you may have, and your previous investment experience. I have listed several key considerations in Part II: "The Whole Tablecloth" (Step 7). If you are at the retirement stage or nearing it, I encourage you to read and reflect on them before you decide on any of the potential strategies. I have also listed many of the key investment products and their features. You'll find them in the section titled "The Good, the Bad, and the Funky."

Distribution Stage

Here you find yourself having led a very good life, but with friends and family members passing away, you feel vulnerable and start to give very serious consideration to passing your wealth on to your heirs. After all, you reckon, you can't take it with you.

The goals most people have at this stage are to minimize the risk and volatility of their investments, preserve their capital, and to minimize taxes and probate costs of their estate. Besides making sure that your will and powers of attorney are up to date, there are strategies you should consider utilizing. Make sure you get professional help so that you can properly understand the consequences of each strategy.

While these strategies may be adopted at various times throughout the Distribution stage, some do have age limits by which they have to be implemented. If you find yourself in the terrible situation of learning that you have a terminal illness, you will be able to utilize some of these strategies with a greater certainty of their benefit.

Also, some of these strategies are not universal from a geographic perspective. For example, Americans cannot pre-gift to the same extent that Canadians can.

Suggested Strategies for the Distribution Phase

Pre-gifting. There's a commercial on television from one of these businesses offering to buy your gold jewellery (caveat: you may only get about 20 cents on the dollar for what it's worth in gold content) that cites various reasons for selling them your gold. One of the reasons is that your children may fight over it. I laugh every time I see that. The old "I'll show you rotten kids. I'll give it away for free before I let either of you have it."

A good way to reduce probate costs and ensure that your loved ones get part of what you intend them to have is to pre-gift them assets or cash before you die. If you're sitting on an investment portfolio where you don't need the income it generates and you are unlikely to need the capital, why not give your children some money now so that they can enjoy it while you're still around? I've often seen where children struggle to make ends meet while a parent hordes cash.

If you need to preserve your assets to provide you with a comfortable lifestyle, then by all means keep them, but if you have more than enough, or if you've been diagnosed with a serious illness and have a feeling that you can see the light just ahead, why not disburse some assets ahead of time.

Holding assets in joint form. Often parents will change their affairs so that they hold bank accounts, homes, cottages, or investment accounts in joint custody with a child. For some people this is a viable strategy for passing assets through to heirs while avoiding probate, but there are many serious problems with structuring your affairs this way, both from a tax perspective and a control perspective, so talk to a professional about the negative consequences before you commit to such a strategy.

> There are two forms of joint ownership. There is Joint-Tenancy-with-Right-of-Survivorship (JTWROS) and there is Tenants-in-Common. If people hold assets in joint form with a right of survivorship, the ownership of the property passes to the remaining owners when one party passes away. Tenants-in-Common, on the other hand, have a specific interest in the asset, and when one of the owners passes away then his or her estate would have title to that portion of the asset. It does not automatically pass to the other persons holding the asset jointly.

Conservative asset mix. Since you are likely interested in preserving your assets for estate purposes, a more conservative asset mix is a prudent strategy. When you're 80 years of age, you usually aren't too concerned about the purchasing power that is being lost by being conservative. Instead, you are more concerned that a drop in the value of your portfolio may not be recoverable within your lifetime.

Insurance-Based Guaranteed Investment Certificates. Also sometimes called Guaranteed Investment Annuities, these investments work just like a GIC that you'd get from a bank, except you get them from an insurance company and you designate a beneficiary on them even if they are non-registered.

When you die, the principal is paid to your beneficiary and bypasses probate and other estate costs.

Maximizing the deposit on your permanent insurance policy. If you have an existing permanent insurance policy, you may have not yet deposited the maximum amount allowed to be contributed under the Maximum Tax Accumulation Reserve (MTAR). This amount grows tax sheltered, but don't just blindly put money into the reserve. Talk to your financial adviser and make sure you are staying within the tax man's rules and that your capital is going to be paid to your heirs.

Estate Guaranteed Investment Funds. Estate GIFs are a form of segregated mutual funds available through insurance companies that offer death benefit protection, protection resets on the growth of the investment, the ability to bypass probate, creditor protection, and flexible investment choices. They are an effective means of passing on an estate, but they come at a cost of a higher management fee.

Inter vivos and Testamentary Trusts. Inter vivos trusts are trusts that are established while you are still alive and testamentary trusts are trusts that are established upon your death. Income earned and retained in inter vivos trusts is taxed at the highest marginal tax rate, whereas income earned and retained in testamentary trusts is taxed on a graduated basis.

Trusts have a role to play for significant estates where you feel the beneficiaries are not capable of handling the financial aspects to your liking; where you want to protect your estate from falling into unwanted hands, such as those of that creepy son-in-law that you never could stand; or where you wish to ensure that they get passed on to later generations long after you are gone.

There is no set age for the distribution stage, but often it takes place in the twilight years of our life. While it may not be cost effective to adopt distribution strategies until this time, you should still give thought as to how you might want to address this stage. Sometimes our health deteriorates, such as in cases of having dementia, and if you wait too long to establish an appropriate strategy, it will be too late or unavailable.

BAPKIN scratch:

Adopt an appropriate retirement strategy based on your life stage, personal situation, and comfort levels. Recognize that there are many different strategies and products available to help you achieve your goals, and understand that no matter what your approach, it will have good and bad attributes but if the good outweighs the bad then you're likely doing okay.

The intention of this chapter was not to make you an expert in retirement strategies but to give you a better idea of what your adviser may be proposing you adopt based on your life stage. Not all advisers are licensed to implement every strategy, so be sure your adviser is capable of providing you with objective advice.

I understand which planning life stage I am in, and have adopted a strategy appropriate to my circumstances: Yes No

Step 8: Have a Disciplined Investment Strategy

Much of this book has been dedicated to describing the process of building and protecting your net worth, but so far little has been written about how to invest your savings. Yet for many of you, this will be the most important function that you will need an adviser to help you with. Why so? That's because the rate of return that you earn on your investments throughout your life is perhaps the most important factor, next to your savings rate, in determining the type of lifestyle you will be able to enjoy.

For example, a $100,000 portfolio invested at 3 percent will be worth about $243,000 in 30 years. If 8 percent is earned, the portfolio would be worth about $1,000,000. That's a sizable range and represents more than four times the standard of living.

Do these differences really occur? They certainly do, and they are a function of asset mix and investor behaviour. The Dalbar Inc. study results for the 20-year period ending December 31, 2009, shows the S&P500 composite index returning an average annual return of 8.2 percent, whereas the average equity investor's return over this same time frame was 3.2 percent.

Let's get into the meat and potatoes of what this step is all about—or perhaps I should say how the table is set for this step, since the meat and potatoes can be found in Part II, where I explain lots of juicy information that I think is important for you to digest at your leisure.

This step involves developing a balanced investment strategy for your savings that will suit your objectives and that you will be able to stick with—meaning you can handle the volatility.

When developing a disciplined investment strategy, the key investment concepts that you need to understand are as follows:

1. The purpose of an Investment Policy Statement
2. Asset allocation
3. Rebalancing
4. Diversification
5. Tactical component
6. Fixed income strategies
7. Equity strategies
8. Investor behaviour
9. Performance measurement

These concepts represent the strategies and tools that most basic portfolio management approaches would include. By understanding why they are important and what they are supposed to achieve, you'll have a better grasp of the potential and safety of your portfolio and the disciplines that you and your adviser should be following.

Investment Policy Statement (The Plan of Action)

Should you happen to make use of professional money management already, you will know about an investment policy statement. An investment policy statement (IPS) is a document that provides the guidelines that your investment manager must follow when managing your account. If you are managing your own portfolio, it is a good idea for you to also make a written statement, at a time that you are not emotional about your investments, that you can review when you have doubts about your investment approach. In essence, you are committing in writing to the principles that you are going to follow in good times and in bad, and by writing them down you are reinforcing them to your subconscious and will likely stay more disciplined.

I can't emphasize enough the importance of being disciplined in your investment approach. *It is the failure to apply your chosen method or methods of investing in a disciplined manner that contributes to poorer performance.*

What's in an investment policy statement? The IPS lists your dominant *financial goals and objectives*, such as whether you are investing for growth, whether you require safety of capital above all, or whether tax minimization is an important necessity. It quantifies the *time horizon* that your capital is going to be invested for, how much *risk you can tolerate*, and what *asset allocation* you feel is appropriate.

Time horizons are important because they influence the level of risk that may be appropriate. If you need your money within a short period, say within five years, then you should stay much more conservative than you otherwise would be considering. But the longer the time horizon, the more time available for your portfolio to recover should the market decide to enter into a bear and so you may be able to handle a higher level of volatility.

Be careful of financial institutions' questionnaires that determine your "appropriate" asset mix, because it has been my experience that as soon as you indicate that the time horizon for your invested capital is longer term, they'll allocate a larger percent to equities than what you may be comfortable with from a short-term volatility perspective.

That's because your financial capacity to handle risk can be greater than your emotional tolerance to handle risk. In my opinion, you either have to take steps to keep your emotional tolerance in check, or else your short-term volatility fears should overrule the higher risk profile that a long-term time horizon is supposed to give you.

> **One size does not fit all!**
>
> At least when it comes to investing.
>
> A 35-year-old male with no dependents has many years before he is going to need his savings to provide retirement income. His IPS may state that because he has 30 years as an investment time horizon and that he is saving for retirement, he is emphasizing growth and is willing to allocate 75 percent of his capital to stocks and 25 percent to bonds and treasury bills. He realizes that his portfolio may suffer negative returns for several years, but he is willing to tolerate that type of volatility, because he feels there is much time and additional savings going into his portfolio to mitigate the damage, and he feels that the equity component will outperform the other classes in the longer-term.
>
> A 45-year-old widow with three children may have a different policy statement. Her IPS may state that she is planning on retirement in 15 years, and because she still has one child in university, she can't afford to put additional savings into her investment portfolio until a few years from now. She is emphasizing income with some growth at this time, since she realizes that she can afford some level of volatility to try to earn higher investment returns, and since it still is 15 years before she's likely to draw any income and so she will allocate 10 percent of her portfolio to cash in case an emergency arises, 60 percent of her portfolio to a fixed income strategy of laddered bonds, and the remainder, 30 percent, to equity mutual funds.

Unfortunately, most investors don't know how much volatility they can truly handle until they are actually experiencing it.

Asset Allocation (The Foundation of Your Portfolio)

Long-term asset allocation is the most important investment decision you will make. That's because if you are broadly diversified and don't keep making timing changes, almost all your overall return can be accounted for based on your long-term asset mix. Just being weighted in the asset class will likely have the largest bearing on your long-term performance rather than individual security selection.

History shows us that equity investments provide a long-term return of about 5 to 7 percent above inflation, while fixed income investments only return 2 to 3 percent above inflation. So why don't we just load up on equity investments and enjoy those great long-term returns?

Well, because they are generated over the long term and not necessarily over the short term. You may not have that long a time frame or you may not have the stomach for the volatility that comes with owning a portfolio consisting solely of stocks.

Volatility is an experienced investor's friend because it creates buying opportunities but less-experienced investors, or those with shorter time horizons, can get scared out of volatile investments, thereby locking in losses and failing to be invested when the market rebounds. Fixed income investments are included in a portfolio in order to smooth out returns and to reduce the volatility. The less volatile, the more likely you are to stay invested and so your returns will be a function of the investment classes that you've allocated capital to over the longer-term rather than your emotional behaviour.

A rule of thumb that can be a starting point for an allocation estimate is to have your age represent the percent that you should have allocated to fixed income. Thus a 30-year-old would have a lower percentage allocated to fixed income (30 percent fixed income, 70 percent equity). You'll recall from the retirement planning step that we adjusted this basic rule of thumb to be more conservative if you were in the acceleration stage or the retirement stage and without a source of guaranteed income. Note that these are only rules of thumb and a starting point. Your personal risk tolerances, time horizons, market experience, and objectives all have an impact on what your allocation should be, with the emphasis being your market experience and your ability to handle volatility and risk. For some, a more aggressive asset mix may be very appropriate.

Your asset mix should not change with market conditions, except for a tactical component that you might have, but it should change with life changes, such as aging. This is a very important discussion to have with your adviser. And don't just use past performance figures to decide on the appropriate asset mix to determine a return objective. Your asset mix should be driven by your risk tolerance so looking at past volatility of the various asset classes, both from a long-term and short-term basis, should give you a better perspective.

Make sure your adviser shows you the downside that can occur although recognize that the steepness of some declines, such as the 2008–2009 correction, is not always foreseeable, nor does it happen very often. I think it's safe to say that I would expect a 10 to 20 percent correction in any given year, in any given stock market, but more sizeable corrections are only foreseeable in environments of very high price/earnings multiples (a valuation concern). Other significant bear markets have occurred in periods of extreme deflation or economic recessions, as in the 1930s, and where there was significant monetary tightening, such as when inflation became rampant in the 1970s, but these are less obvious until they occur.

Rebalancing (A Discipline to Improve Risk-Adjusted Returns)

Part of the asset allocation process is the need to rebalance your investments occasionally so that your asset mix stays within the percent range that you are comfortable with. A discipline of rebalancing periodically, such as annually or when certain percent changes occur, helps you lock in gains on assets that have appreciated and commits more investment capital into those asset classes that have yet to appreciate or that have declined in price and thus you are buying in low.

It's been shown that rebalancing does very little to diminish the long-term returns of a portfolio—in fact, it often increases long-term returns—but it also helps to reduce volatility and lower volatility is the key to staying committed to your investment strategy. Of course, this is easier said than done when markets are going through a volatile correction. Studies show us, though, that persons who stick with a rebalancing discipline have better risk-adjusted returns.

Diversification (A Must!)

Diversification is a necessity. It's sometimes been referred to as the only "free lunch" when investing. I've seen too many times the ravages done to people's lives by persons who fail to diversify. Whether they loaded up on one stock that they thought had a great story, their employer's stock (which they felt they knew the ins and outs of), or an investment class or sector like technology, not being properly diversified permanently wiped out their savings. Remember my couple from Step 1 who invested hugely and solely in Stelco?

Diversification comes in many different forms. Your asset mix is a form of diversification. Geographic diversification can be achieved by investing in markets from all around the world. There are different sectors of the economy, such as health care, resources, and consumer products, and there are different companies within those sectors. There are government bonds, corporate bonds, strip bonds, real return bonds, long-term bonds, short-term bonds—I think you get the point.

There are two main types of risk with investments: *systemic and unsystemic*. Unsystemic risk can be avoided by properly diversifying. It is the risk inherent in each individual security and is also known as "business risk." Any one investment can fall off the face of the earth. It doesn't matter how safe it appears, any single investment can have something go horribly wrong, but being diversified will mitigate any damage that this otherwise would have done to your portfolio. Remember Nortel? It once represented over 35 percent of the Canadian market, and now it is gone.

There is such a thing as over-diversifying. When reflecting on the great academics and investors that have shaped my investment knowledge and philosophies, one theme typically stands out: those that have outperformed the general market have done so by having more concentrated portfolios. The more diversified the portfolios, the more likely they generate market returns. So if you are trying to outperform the market, over-diversification may have detrimental effects on your achieving that goal.

Systemic risk cannot be diversified away except to some degree through asset allocation and having a tactical component. It is the risk one bears when investing in the overall market. If the market enters into a bear phase most security prices fall and no matter where you've invested, your portfolio is likely getting a whupping.

Tactical Component (Not for Everyone but Necessary for Some)

A tactical component is often employed by professionals to try to address the issues with systemic risk and investors' shorter-term investment bias. By having a set percentage of the portfolio able to deviate away from the stated asset mix, the investor tries to time the market somewhat. Since this can defeat the purpose of asset allocation and rebalancing if not done successfully, you or your trusted adviser should have some investing experience and a disciplined "timing" process before I would recommend employing such a technique.

The greatest benefit of having a tactical component is that many investors are emotionally incapable of having a long-term time horizon, so it addresses their "perceived" shorter time horizon. You might not intend or need to use a bucket of investment capital for the next 30 years (see Step 7: "Have a Personal Pension Plan Strategy"), but odds are you will still check the market value each month when you get your statements. Why do we do this? Do we fear losses? Are we greedy and want to gloat over how rich we've become? Are we in continual doubt that what we are doing is right or is the "best" approach? I don't necessarily know, but I do know that our need for continual reinforcement makes us short-term investors even when we needn't be.

So why not accept and embrace our behavioural weakness and allocate a small portion of our portfolio as a tactical investment, and if we get nervous and want to sell the investment and move to cash, then so be it. If it means we'll leave the other monies we have invested alone and properly invest and rebalance them, then it may help our long-term return more than it will hurt it even if we get our timing wrong. After all, it is gut-wrenching for many of us to watch the downward volatility of our hard-earned savings, and the answer isn't to just say, "Relax, fuggedaboutit"; it's to make changes that allow us to sleep at night without damaging our ability to earn acceptable returns.

Can timing work in the long run? Here's an example that I like. In his book *Stocks for the Long Run*, professor Jeremy Siegel demonstrated that using a simple approach of selling an investment representing the Dow Jones Industrial Average each time it fell 1 percent below its 200-day moving average and buying it back again when it rose 1 percent above resulted in achieving a return below the long-run return if the investment was just held and not traded. However through most periods measured it did so with less volatility—and sometimes with a lot less volatility. The question becomes *Was the lower return with the lower volatility a fair trade-off because it is volatility that scares most people out of their long-term investment discipline?'* The answer is *It depends.*

It depends on what period of time you are measuring it from and whether it saved you from some big losses. The approach worked over the very long term (since 1886), and it worked around the great depression (1926 to 1945), and it worked big time in 2008 to 2009.

Does this methodology sometimes not *work?* Dang right. Moving averages or other trend indicators work great when investments are trending up or down, but they fail us when investments trade in a sideways or volatile pattern, often getting us out at a lower price and buying us back in at a higher price. This can happen many times before a trend may develop giving us a series of locked-in losses. In his book, Professor Siegel highlights how the simple technique would have resulted in 16 trades throughout the year 2000 and mini-losses that combined to a total loss of 28 percent, whereas the buy-and-hold investor would have lost only 5 percent that year.

A tactical component can be a good risk management tool for some investors, but it won't always work, and if your system is flawed or you are unlucky you must recognize that your return in the long run may be lower than just following a strategic asset mix approach—and in some cases it can be significantly lower. But I also know that there are many investors who can't stand just sitting there (is that an oxymoron?) watching their investment value go down. I think the secret is to commit only a small portion of your investment capital to a tactical-based approach, enough to satisfy your behavioural demons, and to think of this capital as being in a separate bucket from your other investment assets, which follow a disciplined long-term strategy.

Fixed Income Strategies (Maturity Matters)

There are several fixed income strategies that you can make use of to try to get the most out of your fixed income investments even in a low interest rate environment.

The important thing to understand with fixed income investments, such as bonds and guaranteed investment certificates (GICs), is that the maturity date matters. Typically, the longer the term you decide to lock in for, the higher the yield you get. You should note that there are some periods when this doesn't hold true, but it holds true most of the time.

The other thing to understand is that GICs are one of the few fixed income investments that can't be sold prior to maturity and so don't have a market value. Almost all other fixed income investments can be sold in the marketplace, so they have a market value and that value rises and falls based on a number of factors but mostly because of changes in interest rates. When rates increase, the bonds you own fall in value, and when interest rates decline your bonds will appreciate above and beyond the coupon you receive. The longer the maturity of the bond, the bigger those market value changes are going to be. This can be a good thing or a bad thing when you look at your investment statements.

There are different types of bonds that you can access through individual ownership, mutual funds, and exchange-traded funds (ETFs). These bonds include government bonds, corporate bonds, real return bonds, and high-yield bonds and can be both domestic (the country you live in) or foreign. Because it can be very difficult for a small investor to properly diversify in many of these bond markets, many investors go the mutual fund or ETF route. Bonds usually pay interest twice a year, but some bonds, known as strip bonds or compound bonds, pay interest only at their maturity.

Strategies

If you are going to own individual bonds or GICs, *a bond ladder* is a strategy that you can use to eliminate your need to predict where interest rates might be headed. This can be very attractive to people who feel they can't predict interest rates.

A *barbell strategy* is where you invest part of your money in longer-term bonds in order to earn a higher interest rate and the other part you invest in short-term bonds so that the market value ups and downs are smaller and don't bother you so much.

Because these market values change based on changing interest rates and the length of maturity of the bond, we can try to better our returns by investing in longer-term bonds when interest rates are high and expected to drop, then sell and invest in short-term bonds when interest rates are low and expected to increase. This is known as *duration management* and can be very effective to those who feel they have a crystal ball.

When I talk to clients about fixed income strategies, I like to break down the components into ladder, duration, corporates and high yields, preferred shares, and global bonds. I think it is important that your fixed income strategy either emphasize maximizing income or preserving capital, because even though this component is not usually as volatile as equities, the two objectives aren't met by the same types of fixed income products or strategies.

For those who are interested in learning more, there is much detailed information about fixed income products and strategies found in Part II: "The Whole Tablecloth" (Step 8).

Equity Strategies (Style and Diversification Matters)

As with bonds, there are many different ways that you can invest in equities. Equities are stocks or shares of companies and they represent ownership in the company. As an owner, you are entitled to share in the earnings of the business, including any dividends it might pay. Like fixed income products you can own shares directly, through mutual funds, and through exchange-traded funds. Equities can be domestic or foreign, and if they are foreign, they can be hedged back to your domestic currency, or they can be unhedged, which will provide more opportunities to make money and will of course involve more risks.

> What's the difference between global investments and international investments?
>
> Global investments are from all over the world, including North America, whereas international investments exclude North America.

In order to properly diversify the equity component, you should have enough money to invest in at least 15 to 20 stocks; otherwise, you will be better protected if you make use of mutual funds and ETFs.

There are many different investment styles for equity investing. You can use a value approach or a growth approach, have a dividend emphasis, go with large capitalization stocks, or perhaps even try small capitalization stocks. I make use of all of them.

The BAPKIN Plan calls for you to be diversified by making use of core mutual funds and ETFs and to make use of different investing styles, which should include Canadian and global markets. If you have significant savings and at least $100,000 is going to be put to work in the stock market, then you can consider making use of a professional portfolio manager to invest directly into stocks and perhaps save some money on fees while still having a professional oversee your portfolio. I believe that a combination of high dividend-paying stocks and dividend-growing companies represent one of the best equity strategies for a conservative investor.

There's nothing wrong with having some individual stocks in your equity component if you have less than $100,000, but they should not represent the majority of your portfolio—the ETFs or mutual funds should instead.

I've explained much more about stocks and stock investing strategies in Part II, "The Whole Tablecloth" (Step 8), and I encourage you to read it.

Investor Behaviour (We Are Our Own Worst Enemy)

Your behaviour as an investor is likely to have one of the most significant bearings on your portfolio's performance. I cannot stress this enough.

We all make mistakes when investing, and sometimes we don't make mistakes but we think we do because others do not agree with us or things don't happen the *way* we thought they would happen or *when* we thought they would happen. Stock and bond markets are so dynamic that investing in them can be a very stressful exercise for many people.

There are many different behavioural demons that lurk within us waiting for their moment to cause us to mess up even our best laid plans, but the most important thing to remember is that diversification and sticking with a disciplined investment approach will get you through most of the investing issues and conflicts that will arise during your lifetime.

Once again, I have dedicated more material to the subject in Part II, "The Whole Tablecloth" (Step 8), of this book for those who would like to understand more about this area.

Performance Measurement (It All Comes Down to Perspective and Framing)

In other words, it all comes down to how you look at things. Comparing your performance to particular indices is often an exercise in futility, since it is unlikely that your risk tolerances and investment style matches them and, so it's not conducive to your investment success.

Why? It all comes back to our behaviour. If we aren't doing at least as well as the markets, we often think we are doing something wrong or that our adviser isn't any good. It makes it a lot harder to stick to a disciplined process if we think the process doesn't work anymore, and yet sticking to the discipline is often the most important criteria for success.

> 👍 **THUMPRINT:**
> Build your long-term BAPKIN plan on an expectation (i.e., your goal) somewhere in the range of 3 to 7 percent. That is much more representative of the world as we now know it for balanced portfolios.

You are much better served to compare how you are doing against benchmarks that include investments with fees—such as comparing what quartile ranking your mutual fund falls in; comparing it longer-term against a no-fee, no-risk investment, such as Guaranteed Investment Certificates: or better yet, using the BAPKIN way—comparing it against a "goal-based" return dependent on your asset mix and current market conditions, just like pension plans do.

> 👍 **THUMBPRINT**
> Whether you are a novice or seasoned investor, I encourage you to read the detailed material relevant to this step found in Part II, "The Whole Tablecloth." It's chock full of practical information that will make you much more knowledgeable regarding your investments and investment strategies, and hopefully it will help you be a lot more successful and comfortable with your plan.

BAPKIN scratch:

Be balanced, properly diversified, and consistent in your investment approach. Understand investment concepts and strategies and adopt a strategy that meets your tolerance for risk, first and foremost, and then stick with it.

Different styles and approaches will take their turns being the better place to be. Understand that all investment products and strategies have good things and bad things about them, so make use of the ones that have more good than bad based on your objectives. Use an appropriate benchmark to monitor your progress so that you will limit behavioural demons.

I have a balanced portfolio and know my desired asset mix: Yes No

I understand and agree with the investment strategies that I am using …

for fixed income: Yes No

for growth: Yes No

I am using an appropriate benchmark (such as a "goal-based" return of 3 to 7 percent) to evaluate my long-term progress: Yes No

STEP 9: YOUR FINANCIAL ADVISER IS HERE TO HELP YOU

I went to the local fish and chip shop to get supper one night. I asked the order taker for an order of fish and chips. "Halibut or haddock?" she asked. "I don't know," says I. "What's the difference?"

"Oh, honey," says she, "if you don't know the difference, just get the haddock!"

While advisers are not fish, many investors do feel they are all alike. But they definitely are not! Here are some things to think about when selecting a financial adviser to work with.

Dealing with a Financial Professional

I once did an informal survey asking people just what they expected when dealing with a professional, be it a doctor, a lawyer, an accountant, or a financial adviser. I thought it an interesting exercise, because each profession has its service code and code of ethics, and I wondered how people would relate their experience and expectations dealing with the various professions.

There were attributes common among the professions, but there seemed to be a fairly large gap between the expectations people had and how they felt their experience with advisers had been. I originally thought that this was because of differences in education.

In the financial field, advisers must be licensed to provide advice, and there is the requirement for continuing education each year, but unlike the other professions, there are minimal requirements to have professional designations. Among the designations that do exist, not all are equal. Some are very difficult to achieve and require significant years of experience before they are granted. There are also different licenses that financial advisers must be qualified for if they are going to provide investment advice regarding different investment products such as mutual funds, stocks and bonds, insurance products, discretionary portfolio management services, and options, but most advisers do not have all these licenses.

Are high-net-worth investors a little more attuned to the advisery world? A survey done about 10 years ago on behalf of the CFA Institute found that the financial credentials most recognized by high-net-worth investors were the Chartered Accountant (CA) in Canada (or Certified Public Accountant [CPA] in the United States), the Certified Financial Planner (CFP), and Chartered Financial Analyst (CFA) designations. These designations are very difficult to achieve, requiring hundreds of hours of study and years of practical experience, and they have strict code of ethics that their members must follow.

But even among these financial professionals, they all have different expertise. Accountants are great at tax issues but are not trained or licensed to give specific investment advice. Often their personal experience is the extent of their investment knowledge. Persons with Chartered Financial Analyst designations might be great at investment strategies and security selection, but they are not educated and qualified to provide estate planning advice. Certified Financial Planners might be best qualified to provide general financial planning advice but each adviser's experience and specialty differs. These differences would certainly imply why such a large expectations gap appears to exist.

An unnerving theme that arose in my discussions was that persons who were doing well with their investments generally felt that their adviser was doing a good job, but if the investments were not doing well, they doubted whether the adviser was competent. This was confirmed in a survey that was done by J. D. Power and Associates in 2009, which found that a significant percent of investors felt less loyal to their advisers after going through the most recent bear market, as if it were the advisers' fault.

This soon became apparent as one of the main reasons for the expectations gap, and it can sometimes be a completely unfair assessment of the adviser, but it is a reality. A friend who is a chartered accountant once told me that he didn't envy what I did because I was always being judged as to whether I was doing a good job or not. Of course the criteria that most people use would be their performance, and because this industry is as much a sales industry as it is a service industry, there is always a competitor saying he would have done things differently and better—with the benefit of hindsight, I might add.

Evaluating an Adviser

So what qualities should you look for when evaluating your adviser, asking someone for a referral, or meeting with an adviser or a financial coach for the first time?

The following can serve as a checklist for many of the attributes you should be looking for:

- *Client focussed.* They care about you and helping you meet your needs and goals.
- *Experience.* They have diverse experience or specialize in the area you want to use their services and have access to other professionals.
- *Conservative.* Most investors prefer an adviser who is conservative over one who is aggressive in their recommendations; your chosen adviser should understand your definition of risk and should incorporate that into your relationship.
- *Qualified.* The adviser should have an appropriate educational background and licensing.
- *Personable.* You want your interaction to be enjoyable.

- *Fair pricing.* Don't make cost a criteria; make it value instead.
- *Integrity.* You especially want to look for signs that the adviser is ethical, trustworthy, and objective. Signs that an adviser does not have integrity is if he guarantees investment returns on non-guaranteed investments like mutual funds, if he asks you to partake in private loans to his business, if he leads you to expect returns much higher than our 3 to 7 percent rule of thumb for a balanced portfolio, or if he continually wants to trade investments in your portfolio.
- *Professionalism.* When was the last time a veterinarian, doctor, accountant, or lawyer approached you and tried to convince you that they were better than the professional you were currently using? Professionals don't do that—it's against their code of ethics—but salespeople do. It's up to you if you want to deal with a professional or with a salesperson in the financial services field.

Communicating with Your Adviser

In addition to the qualities listed above, communication is important. The adviser should have a systemic means of communicating with you, including phone calls, e-mails, newsletters, and portfolio reviews. While I think of it, never trust a handwritten statement from an adviser or his word that the back office statements are incorrect—it's a sign of improper conduct. Many investors do not understand how to read their investment statements, and this can lead to investor uncertainty. If you don't know how to read your statements or portfolio evaluations, don't be embarrassed. You are not in the minority. Just call up your adviser or his assistant and ask him to talk you through the first few that you receive.

Remember, the idea is to simplify and improve your life, so when choosing an adviser to work with, be sure you are comfortable with that person. He or she should be objective and capable of investing your money in a wide variety of products. How do you ensure that he's objective? That's difficult but as a rule of thumb, the fewer products that an adviser has available, the less likely it is that he will be objective.

If you want to be doing financial planning, even in this book's basic form, your adviser should have a financial planning designation and experience or access to it. Not all advisers who call themselves "planners" have their Certified Financial Planner designation and the related experience that must be achieved to obtain the designation.

If you are unsure that the advice you are being provided is appropriate or best suited for you, consider paying a fee-based adviser to provide a second opinion review. This adviser should not be potentially handling your investments or else it puts his or her objectivity in question. For about $500, the objectivity provided could save you thousands and even tens of thousands of dollars. The problem with most institutions that advertise offering a second opinion is that you can't really trust their advice. That's because they have an agenda, and that agenda is to get your business, so you know they are going to criticize what your adviser has done, and often this criticism is very unfair and even misleading. What I find comical is that the advisers providing the second opinion are often less qualified than the investor's existing adviser.

You can also consider hiring a coach for your financial journey. A financial coach is a fee-based adviser who can help guide you in your decision making. You pay for the adviser's time, wisdom, and experience, but you are ultimately responsible for the final decision and management of your financial affairs. It's like hiring a consultant.

Meeting Your Financial Goals

If you are going to make use of a financial adviser, that person can only help you properly if you disclose your financial situation in its entirety. Holding back can lead to her being misinformed and not evaluating your situation properly.

You'll need to set clear goals for yourself and communicate them to your adviser. If you have significant changes in your life, such as getting married, having a baby, buying a property, getting divorced, or being offered a new job somewhere, let your adviser know so she can update your profile and perhaps parts of your plan need to be adjusted.

Your adviser is happy to stay in touch with you and you can communicate through personal visits, the telephone, and even e-mail. Most of what needs to be done when updating plans and managing your money does not require a personal visit unless you want it to. You don't have to wait for a scheduled meeting to contact your adviser. She wants to be involved in your life and well-being. Your adviser may also communicate to you through information provided on her website, in a personal newsletter, or perhaps written or video updates done on a quarterly basis.

Let your adviser know what your expectations are from a communication perspective and your adviser will let you know what he expects of you. Remember, your adviser does not have to have you as a client if he or she doesn't want to. You are entering into a business relationship where both parties have to want to be in it together in order for it to work best.

Lastly, have reasonable expectations and realize that your adviser can only do so much within the realm of investing. His job is to match your objectives and your tolerance for risk and volatility with the investment products that exist. Sometimes the performance may be lacking, but if proper diversification and investment management techniques are being applied then it's unlikely that any other adviser would have done you any better and may possibly have done worse.

This reminds me of another story. I had a client and a friend who was constantly being prospected by an adviser who kept telling him that he could do much better than I was doing. We had invested conservatively and were slowly getting the client accustomed to mutual fund investments because he lacked market experience, and our five-year performance figure was around 8.2 percent.

Since my friend kept getting pestered, I told him to ask the adviser to send a sample portfolio. I figured I'd at least be able to see how the other adviser proposed to invest my client's money. When we saw the portfolio, it was comprised of mutual funds and individual stocks—the "core and explore" technique—and the stocks appeared to be good ones at the time. I say "at the time" because the two that I remember were Nortel and Bombardier, both of which have since imploded.

While looking at the portfolio, my friend looked at the bottom right-hand corner and said to me, "What's this? Five year CAGR 7.8 percent?" I chuckled. The 7.8 percent was the portfolio's *actual* five-year compound annual growth rate, and it was lower than the 8.2 percent that we had achieved. So my caveat is to beware promises—most advisers who have the attributes of a professional don't make them when it comes to performance.

> 👍 **THUMBPRINT**
>
> Don't invest with an adviser because he gave you a high estimate when you asked what type of expected return he thinks he can earn you. An estimate means nothing, and advisers may quote higher numbers than what may be likely just to win your business.

Consolidating Investments with One Adviser

Consolidating your assets with one adviser is sometimes necessary in order to get lower pricing, and it definitely makes the planning and monitoring of your portfolio much easier to evaluate. The quality of your adviser's advice can be greatly improved if the adviser can continually see how everything is doing and how it is integrated and allocated.

Consolidation is absolutely necessary if your adviser is going to try to make things more tax efficient. It can simplify the preparation of your tax return, because your accountant will only have to deal with one adviser who can provide him with a gain/loss summary and can make sure that you have received all your appropriate tax slips. If you have investments spread all over, the gain/loss summary may not be accurate, because you may have a different adjusted cost base for tax purposes than what is at your adviser's firm. Not all advisers or their assistants are equal in knowledge here. Your adviser and his assistant need to understand the various slips that get generated for tax purposes, including the ones that aren't generated at his investment firm but instead are generated from a mutual fund company or some other source, as well as the information that doesn't get generated, such as the interest on strip bonds.

All that said, the choice to consolidate is yours. Perhaps you like to use specialists for insurance, investment management, and estate planning. That can be effective. Perhaps you want to keep various personal and business relationships and like the idea of diversifying amongst portfolio managers. That too can be effective. It depends what your objectives are. The important thing to note is that a financial adviser cannot properly advise you without knowing your financial situation, and by using several different advisers, you introduce the potential to receive conflicting advice and it will be up to you to decide which advice is most trustworthy.

If you use competing advisers you may also introduce an environment where the less professional advisers will *purposely* criticize what the other advisers are doing in order to plant doubt in your mind and hopefully win over more of your business. These criticisms are sometimes petty or unfair, and it will be left up to you to decide if the conflict and continual doubt is worth it. I've never yet found where it is, and unfortunately it is the better salesman who is often the victor. Beware the salesman. I've often seen investors going to advisers who tell them what they want to hear rather than to advisers who tell them more realistic expectations, and the investor is the loser in the end.

BAPKIN scratch:

Don't be afraid to work with a qualified, objective adviser who is on your side. Consider consolidating your assets. Use this book as a reference to understand the rationale for your adviser's recommendations.

I have considered whether I need to work with a financial adviser: Yes No

I have considered whether I need to consolidate my assets: Yes No

Conclusion to Part I

If you've read this far, you're already on the right path to financial empowerment. You've learned the basic steps to take to start down that path. And your mind may already be working on solving the financial issues that face you.

As a quick reminder, here's a summary of the steps that are written on the back of the napkin.

1. **Have a commitment to living a better life.** In order to have a better life, have a commitment to setting simple goals and to following a simple plan based on common sense. Have a savings target that you are going to work toward. For most people it's somewhere between $300,000 and $900,000. Have no debt when you retire.

2. **Live within your means.** That includes having a component for savings. Learn to save by paying yourself first!

3. **Draft up a statement of net worth.** Revisit it every year. Use it to make decisions which emphasize buying assets that are capable of appreciating and that result in reducing debt. That's how wealth grows!

4. **Protect yourself.** There are various insurances to protect many different things that can go wrong and put a wrench in your wealth-creation efforts.

5. **Protect your loved ones.** Have life insurance coverage, a will, and powers of attorney. Maintain a list of assets, creditors, and people or institutions with whom you deal.

6. **Understand how you are taxed.** Get professional help in understanding what you should be doing. You should have a basic knowledge of how the tax system works and how to reduce taxes using the 3 Ds and 3 Cs.

7. **Have a personal pension plan strategy, based on your stage in life.** If you don't have vast amounts of wealth, you may need to guarantee income for life.

8. **Have a disciplined investment strategy.** Make sure it suits your objectives and you will be able to stick with it. It must satisfy your emotional ability to handle volatility and risk. The focus should be on your asset mix, diversification, and making use of different investment styles. You need to have an appropriate way to measure if you're on track.

9. **Work with the adviser who is the professional—not the salesman.** A suit or a big-name institution doesn't designate professionalism: credentials and integrity do. Think about consolidating for tax-efficiency purposes (but only if with a trusted expert) or making use of a fee-based wealth management coach.

This wraps up the basic components of the BAPKIN Plan. Congratulations on learning many important concepts, for taking the steps, and for making the decisions that so many other people merely procrastinate over. I hope you are feeling liberated by the steps you have already taken and I encourage you to keep moving forward.

There is more to learn if you are willing. In the next section—Part II, "The Whole Tablecloth"—I have provided much more detail and information, so much so that we spilled it over the entire tablecloth. I have also included a financial decision-making framework called a balanced DIET to help you decide what to do if you are having a difficult time making a financial decision.

In the final section—the Appendix—I have provided some blank forms to help you prepare your household statement of net worth, cash flow statement, and a life insurance needs analysis.

I wish you the best of luck in your creating wealth and a better life!

PART II: THE WHOLE TABLECLOTH

For those readers who want to go further in your BAPKIN Plan, Part II, "The Whole Tablecloth" is for you. It contains more detailed information about money management, investing, and pension plans, along with additional strategies and investment options to consider. So, Beyond the Napkin ...

Step 1: Beyond the Napkin—A Better Life

Going beyond the napkin, implementing a cash management plan for yourself will be a crucial early step. Cash management is a fancy way of saying "create a savings program and a debt reduction strategy," and it is the cornerstone to any wealth-creation program. Here are four action areas that you should adapt as a matter of routine throughout your life.

- Save a percentage of income.
- Reduce or eliminate debt.
- Substitute "bad" debt with "good" debt.
- Set up a record-keeping system.

Save a Percentage of Income

As already explained, the most important action that you must do is to immediately put aside part of your take-home pay each pay period as part of a savings program. Don't get me wrong; it always sounds easier than it is to do, but it is imperative that you do it and learn to live within your means.

What do you do with your savings? It doesn't have to go into an investment. It can be used to pay down debt also. If you make your normal mortgage and debt payments (car loans, credit cards, etc.) and then use a 10 to 15 percent figure to save for retirement or pay down debt faster then you'll have a good discipline that will enable you to build on a foundation.

You need an investment program, even if it's a small one, in order to get the benefits of compound growth and to get experience with handling investments. I don't recommend doing one approach (i.e., paying down debt or investing your savings) at the exclusivity of the other. Though the math may work out favouring debt reduction over guaranteed investments while in the savings mode, I've seen where people concentrate on paying down their mortgage as fast as possible and then in the end, when they start their savings program, there might only be 15 years left of saving and investing.

This is hardly enough time to get the true benefits of compound growth, as was evidenced in Figure 2-1. People also tend to be more conservative investors later in life and with limited investment experience will likely not be able to handle very much volatility, nor will they be able to invest in potentially better performing investments, such as common stocks. This makes it difficult for you to invest in a manner that will provide an appropriate rate of return. What type of lifestyle would you have if you inherited some money or decided to look after your own pension monies and didn't have investment experience? It could be very stressful to you.

People tend to not commit the same amount of savings to their investment program as they do to their debt repayment, because they find other areas to spend the money. Once mortgage free, they feel they have sacrificed for long enough and instead save a smaller amount than they ever allocated to their mortgage and spend more on current consumption. So don't ignore a savings/investment program. It's a discipline that you need to embed in your psyche.

Does it make sense to borrow money to invest? I'm not a fan of leveraging that way, because investing can be a very emotional experience, and leveraging just makes the feelings more intense. In order to write off the interest on an investment loan, there must be a risk involved with the investment, and that can compound a bad situation.

Be that as it may, my own rule of thumb for borrowing is that, providing you can tolerate the risk, it's okay to borrow in order to acquire an asset capable of appreciating, such as a home or an investment portfolio, but borrowing for depreciating assets or expenses, such as automobiles and holidays, should be done in moderation.

> 👍 **THUMBPRINT**
>
> If you're going to borrow, do so to acquire assets that are capable of appreciating, such as real estate and investments. If you are borrowing to acquire assets that depreciate over time or are expenditures, such as a holiday, then do so in moderation and on a very limited basis.

Reduce or Eliminate Debt

Now when it comes to debt, there is good debt and there is bad debt, but there is usually debt throughout a major part of our lives. You are more than likely aware of the magic of compounding investment returns, but you should realize that debt has the opposite effect. It is a powerful wealth destroyer. Therefore, it should be a top priority to reduce debt as quickly as possible. For example, by repaying even just $200 extra from your mortgage each month, you can save thousands of dollars in interest over the life of a mortgage and will be able to save and invest more once the debt has been eliminated.

The great thing about paying down debt is that it is a guaranteed return and it is almost always at a higher rate than guaranteed investments, such as bonds and GICs. There have been times in the past where interest rates have been so high it is a slam dunk to pay debt off, because returns from investments just can't compete, especially on a guaranteed basis. And certain types of debt, such as department store and credit card debt, is at such a high rate they dwarf likely investment returns. So do the math. If the rate you are paying on a loan is high, say, 6 percent or greater, then concentrate on paying down debt more so than investing.

> **THUMBPRINT**
>
> If the rate you are paying on a loan is 6 percent or greater, then concentrate on paying down that debt more so than investing.

Substitute "Bad" Debt with "Good" Debt

If you are going to have to incur debt, do your best to make it tax deductible so that the interest cost is somewhat subsidized by the government. This might involve selling some investment assets to pay off a non-deductible debt, such as a car loan, and then borrowing to invest into other investment assets that enable the deduction of interest costs. Tax laws are different everywhere and are constantly changing, so talk to your accountant if you think that you have an opportunity to juggle things around to your advantage. I can't stress this enough. There have been a few recent court cases challenging this area, so you need to talk to someone whose knowledge is current.

If you have high-cost debt, such as credit cards with balances outstanding at exorbitant rates, like 18 percent, talk to your bank about getting a consolidation loan so that the interest cost will be much lower. Of course, if you do consolidate then you must stop using your credit card, or you'll just dig yourself into a deeper hole.

Here's a quick tip: if you are constantly running a balance on your credit card that you can't repay each month, then you are living beyond your means. *Stop* and get help from a credit counsellor. There are persons out there who are trained to help people who have issues with spending and controlling their debt levels.

Be careful, though. Some credit counsellors are merely debt consolidators who charge a high fee for juggling your payments amongst your creditors and keeping them from harassing you each month. They don't necessarily help you in refinancing and paying down your debts. Talk to your adviser, accountant, or lawyer if you need a creditable referral.

Set Up a Record-Keeping System

If you're gung-ho, continue to track your income and expenses each month using financial software, such as Quicken. Your spending patterns will change as you go through your personal life stages. Record keeping can help you prioritize where holes may develop in your savings and wealth-creation program.

Whether you use a computer software program or a pencil-and-paper system, the point is to track your money. That way you're able to keep an eye on expenses and not let things get out of hand.

> *Don't save what is left after spending; spend what is left after saving.*
>
> —Warren Buffett

Step 5: Beyond the Napkin— Protect Your Loved Ones

Here are some factors to consider when deciding on the types and how much insurance to buy. There are several types of life insurance, and while they all serve the purpose of estate creation and preservation, some also provide additional benefits. In addition, cost may be a factor for you in your decision making.

> 👍 **THUMBPRINT**
>
> Life insurance—get it while you can and get it while it's cheap! In other words, get it while you are healthy and young. I usually recommend you get serious about getting permanent insurance when in your thirties or forties. But if you're much older and married, you might still be able to get a joint-and-last-to-die policy for your heirs (not you or your spouse) at a reasonable price. It doesn't hurt to ask your adviser to get a quote.

Term Insurance

As the name suggests, term insurance is insurance that covers your life for a given period of time. Term periods vary—5, 10, and 20 years being the most popular terms. Term insurance is the purest form of insurance. There are no bells or whistles. For this reason, it is also the cheapest insurance, especially in your younger years. As you age, this type of insurance rises in cost, because the older you get the more likely you are to die and the insurance company will have to pay out to your beneficiaries.

For many people, their only life insurance is a form of group insurance from their employer. This insurance is term insurance. You've got it as long as you're an employee, but it disappears once you retire, get terminated, or quit, so failure to have any other insurance policy may leave you high and dry at a time when you need it most.

If you are going with a personal term policy, it is best to ensure that you have renewable and convertible clauses. A *renewable* clause means that you can renew the insurance without having to go through another medical. A *convertible* clause means that you can convert the policy to another form of policy, such as whole life, should you choose to, but it will be more expensive than if you had just gone with a permanent policy to begin with. Without such clauses, you may find that the insurance company refuses to issue you another policy once you let them know that you've been struck by some potentially fatal illness or should you otherwise become uninsurable.

Term insurance will only be available to you while you are younger. Most insurers eliminate coverage on people anywhere from ages 65 to 80, depending on the insurer, so its value as a financial legacy creator has an expiration date.

T100 or Term-to-100

This is my insurance of choice for the middle classes and it's basically a term insurance policy with a guarantee of insurability under the term platform until you are age 100.

The T100 policy is good for those who know they need insurance well after the kids have grown up and moved on. You may own property that has appreciated over time such as an investment portfolio, a business, or a cottage, and these investments may have significant tax liabilities due upon death. Rather than having your executor dispose of the property in order to pay off the taxes, you may choose to have life insurance to cover the tax liability, leaving your beneficiary the ability to receive the property intact.

So how do the premiums on a term-to-100 policy compare to regular term insurance?

The premiums on a T100 policy are more expensive in the early years relative to a regular term policy because the insurance company calculates how much you will need to pay for the insurance through your lifetime and then charges a flat rate throughout the insurable term. Thus you are pre-paying to some extent, part of the higher insurance costs that would be incurred later in your life. But this isn't necessarily a bad thing, because it lets you spread out the higher costs that will be incurred in the later years, making it more affordable than renewing a series of terms in the long run. Also, your estate will have something to show for all the premiums you paid, which isn't the case for term insurance, which runs out at some point.

Universal Life Insurance

Variable insurance, also known as universal life, is a form of insurance that allows you to contribute additional monies into the policy besides the cost of the insurance. This amount, which is above and beyond your premium, is what we often refer to as a side fund, and it can earn investment income that is sheltered from tax as long as it stays in the side fund or is used to pay the premiums. Sounds great, I know, except you will often have limited investment choices, and they typically have high fees and low yields associated with them. Still, if you're tax sensitive and have lots of spare cash floating around, it is an option.

By being a variable policy, your return will vary based on your investment portfolio's outcome. If you do poorly, your side fund will go down in value. Do well and it appreciates. The insurance protection itself lasts your lifetime provided you keep paying the premiums.

Whole Life

The last of the insurance types that I want to discuss is whole life. It's like variable insurance, except the insurance company does the investing selection for you and you share in the experience gains or losses of the insurance company. It's typically a more expensive form of insurance, but some people prefer the convenience of not having to deal with investment decision making, and the experience rating gains may provide some additional decent returns to your portfolio.

> 👍 **THUMBPRINT**
>
> If you are wealthy and in a high tax bracket, life insurance can be a tax-effective investment. By all means make use of whole life or universal life policies if you can afford them. If you fall in the lower-to-middle class income levels, a term-to-100 policy is usually the most cost effective and gives you permanent coverage.

My bottom line on life insurance: Get it while you can and get it while it's cheap! Get it while you are healthy and get it while you are younger, which for most people *is* when they are healthy. If you are in a higher tax bracket, universal life and whole life have tax-savings advantages, but for most persons who are lower and middle-class income level, a term-to-100 policy is my favoured vehicle.

Coverage: How Much Should You Have?

When determining how much life insurance you need, there are three pools that need to be determined. The first is the amount of capital that your survivors are going to need to settle lump-sum cash payments that arise at your death, such as funeral expenses, debts to pay off, estate expenses, and taxes that may arise. The second is the capital that will be required in the future for significant expenses, such as university education costs for your children. The third pool is the amount of capital that your survivors will require in order to provide an income supplement to replace your income.

I know you'll probably want a quick and dirty rule of thumb, and if I was pushed to it I would suggest $300,000 to $700,000 for most middle-class persons, but really, because there is a cost to insurance, you should look at your personal situation and do a proper needs analysis.

> 👍 **THUMBPRINT**
>
> Most middle-class people fall within a $300,000 to $700,000 range of insurance need, and that includes what they would like to leave to their heirs. Think it seems high? If you are 40 today and estimate that your demise may come when you are 85, a $500,000 policy paid out to your children will be equivalent to paying them $165,000 in today's dollars assuming a 2.5 percent inflation rate.

A factor to consider when deciding on the amount of life insurance you want to carry is ensuring you have enough coverage to cover all the family debts, not just your own. After all, you don't want your loved ones to have to be paying for any debts that may have accumulated at a point when they no longer have your income to help pay the bills. You'll want to cover your burial costs and a lump sum to cover expenses while the family grieves, as well as an amount to provide investment income to replace the income your family will be losing with you no longer working. If your loved ones are likely to have significant capital outlays in the future, such as going to university, then there too is a capital amount that you will need to provide for.

When you go see your financial adviser, he or she should be filling out a schedule similar to the one at the end of this Beyond the Napkin step, called a *life insurance needs analysis*, in order to help determine how much insurance is appropriate. If there is a shortfall of savings to cover your needs, you will need insurance to cover the difference.

Three last things about life insurance: (1) It's usually received tax free, an advantage to cost-effective estate creation and preservation for your family. (2) While it is best to get it while you are healthy and young, it can be quite cost-effective to get it while you are married, even if you are older, on the basis that it will be paid out to your heirs after both yours and your spouse's death. This is known as a joint-and-last-to-die policy. (3) In my experience, people don't feel they need insurance or want it until it is too late to get. I've found that many people, once they have aged and accumulated assets, are upset that much of their estate can disappear to taxes and fees when they pass away leaving substantially less behind than they hoped. I recommend that you have a personal life insurance policy that will last for life. It will provide much greater peace of mind when you are older and will provide flexibility when determining retirement income needs and estate concerns. You'll feel less guilty spending the money you saved if you know there is an estate value safe in place.

Don't put off getting life insurance. By all means, let cost be a factor, but I don't think your intention is to leave your loved ones destitute or scratching out an existence should life throw you a curveball. Life insurance is the answer for many a financial problem, but I'll reemphasize what I've already said: get it while you are able, get it while it is cheap—preferably in your thirties or forties, heck even your fifties—and make sure you have it for life.

> **Have the kids pay!**
>
> Getting on in years and feel you can no longer afford paying the premiums on your permanent insurance policy? What you can do is have the beneficiaries of your policy take over paying your premiums, especially if they have become well established and can afford it more than you can. They can always view it as part of their retirement savings program.

It's all in the "math"!

Need further encouragement to get a personal permanent insurance plan in place?

Look at it as another savings program for the benefit of your heirs. Below is a summary for a 50-year old male, Term-to-100 policy. If the guy lives to 100, the insurance company will pay out his insurance so it's not like short-term term insurance which is a sunk cost.

The insurance is received tax-free to his heirs so it makes sense to compare the rate of return on a pre-tax basis assuming a 35% average tax rate.

"Guy" lives until age	Rate of Return	How much would you have to earn in a GIC or bond to be comparable?	What can you earn on a Government of Canda bond for this time frame?	
100 *	2.50%	3.85%		Likely worth it!
90	4.11%	6.32%		Worth it!
81	6.76%	**10.40%**	3.41%	**Definitely worth it!**
60	46.88%	**72.12%**	2.72%	**Definitely worth it!**

* this is the worst case scenario from an "investment" point of view. I'm pretty sure Guy will be happy to be alive as long as his quality of life is good.

Example as of August 27/2010

The BAPKIN Plan

How much life insurance do you need?

First Capital Pool - cover your current expenses

1. There's administrative costs associated with dying. Funeral costs, legal and excutors fees will add up. $ 15,000

2. Probate fees are going to range from 0% to 1.5% 2,000

3. There will also be income taxes. When you die, it's as if you sold everything for tax purposes, if it isn't transferred to your spouse. Estimate your income taxes that may be incurred - don't forget big items like the cottage. 10,000

4. Clear off all your debts. If you haven't utilized your financial institutions' group life insurance for loans and mortgages, then account for them here:

Mortgage	$ 150,000	
Car loan	13,000	
Line of credit	-	163,000

5. Assuming you're a pretty good guy or gal, there's going to be grieving for you. It will be hard for your spouse to work for awhile. Provide some emergency capital for your loved ones to get by on so that they don't have to worry about day-to-day expenses. 10,000

Current expense capital required: $ 200,000

6. Second Capital Pool - Future expense required - University costs 50,000

Total of first and second capital pools: $ 250,000

Total of first and second capital pools: $ 250,000

Third Capital Pool - replacing your income

7. Not all expenses will disappear or be reduced if you were to die. Property taxes, heat and hydro are examples of expenses that are not likely to change much, if at all. But food and other expenses are likely to be reduced. Estimate how much income your family will need each month to maintain an appropriate lifestyle (a rule of thumb would be about 40% less than you need now).

Monthly income	$ 7,000
8. Reduce this amount by your spouse's income	(3,000)
9. This is the net monthly income required	4,000
10. Now we have to factor in income taxes. They'll need about 35% more of this income $ 4,000 x 1.35	$ 5,400

11. Assuming your loved ones can earn 2.5% above inflation, divide the required additional income by a factor of .025
Future income capital required: $ 5,400 / .025   216,000

Total capital pool required: $ 466,000

Where's this money going to come from?

12. You've likely got some sources of capital already squirreled away or established.

(a) Group life insurance through work ***	$ 200,000
(b) Personal life insurance	-
(c) Cash in your bank accounts including your emergency fund	15,000
(d) Investments that can be sold or can provide income	100,000
(e) Registered accounts that will be cashed-in.	-

Total capital that you will already have $ 315,000

Additional insurance required: $ 151,000

*** Note: If you are doing this exercise in order to get personal insurance to replace insurance that you have through work then don't include the group insurance in your calculation.

Step 7: Beyond the Napkin—Have a Personal Pension Plan Strategy

For your pension plan, the decisions that go beyond the napkin include commuting a pension and understanding retirement income investments.

Commuting Your Pension

One of the factors in your personal pension plan strategy is the question of commuting.

Yes, I'm aware of just how much many people hate commuting to work in major urban centres, but that's not what this section is about.

An important consideration that arises at the retirement stage is whether you should commute your pension. "Commuting" means transferring your pension assets from your employer's care to your own, and it's a decision you have to make when you leave your employment or retire. The answer often lies in the type of pension that you have. A defined-contribution plan is usually worth commuting to the adviser of your choice, since there is usually no advantage to keeping the money with your employer's chosen institution. A defined-benefit plan, however, is a lot harder to determine.

> 👍 **THUMBPRINT**
>
> It is usually beneficial to commute a defined-contribution pension or group RRSP to your chosen financial adviser.

It's important to understand all that your company pension plan has to offer, including whether it is indexed for inflation and whether there are any medical benefits that you may be entitled to when you are retired. If you commute your defined-benefit pension, you will likely lose these benefits. If your adviser is pressuring you to commute your defined-benefit pension, think twice and get an unbiased second opinion. I can't stress this point enough. Some advisers will sometimes entice you with unrealistic rates of return and will ignore the advantages of inflation-indexing.

Another risk of commuting a defined-benefit pension is that some of the capital may become immediately subject to taxation due to restrictions in the income tax act. The effect is that you are left with less money to transfer and a lower pension.

> **Benefit or contribution?**
>
> It is very important that you understand the type of pension plan that you have at work. A defined-*benefit* pension plan is one that provides you with a guaranteed pension income based on your years of service and the wages that you earned. This is the type of pension that teachers, government workers, and hospital workers have, but it is becoming rare to see one amongst other employers. With this pension plan, the employer assumes the risk of investing and will have to put more money into the plan if there isn't enough to satisfy the pension obligations.
>
> A defined-*contribution* plan is what the majority of people have got. It's basically a group RRSP. Here the employer just contributes a certain amount each year, and it's up to the employee to select good investments, usually from a limited selection. If the investments do poorly, that's the employee's problem, as no further employer obligations are to be had. These pensions are usually worth commuting.

I remember a local financial planning firm advertising in the late 1990s for teachers to attend "workshops" (teachers love workshops) preaching the need for them to commute their pensions, on the premise that they would have to forego their capital to the Teachers' Pension Plan when they and their spouse passed away rather than have the remaining value go to their children.

The teachers who attended these "workshops" were impressed with the presentations and the return projections that went along with them, so much so that many of them went ahead and commuted their pensions. The return projections were based on historical data emphasizing global mutual funds, which had a phenomenal run from 1978 through 1998, and these returns were somewhat aided by the decline of the Canadian dollar. When I pointed out to one client that most retired persons would not have such a heavy allocation to global equities, and that in any case such returns were not normal, I was told emphatically by that client that I was wrong. I can still remember him saying to me in a very arrogant tone, "Well, you're wrong!"

At that time, I recommended that teachers not commute their pension. The Ontario Teachers' Pension is considered the holy grail by pension standards, and there was no way that a person could achieve the returns necessary to provide a comparable pension without assuming more risk than what most retired investors would be comfortable with.

I have heard that some of the teachers who had commuted had to go back to work part-time because of the money that they had lost when the global markets crumbled in 2000. Heaven only knows what these poor people are left with now that they've been drawing on their capital for 10 years and endured another gut-wrenching correction in the markets as well as the appreciation of the Canadian dollar. Returns on global investments, stated in terms of Canadian dollars, are still negative after 10 years. A rough lot in life all because the teacher who commuted considered his or her pension a financial legacy rather than a retirement income.

Key Considerations to Your Retirement Strategy

There are other factors to consider in your pension plan strategy. At the retirement stage, you've likely built up a significant nest egg, but what you do with it will have an important bearing on your lifestyle for the next 30 years. Here are some key considerations that are going to have an impact on the strategy that you choose to follow.

Variable and Sequential Risk

Simply put, sequential risk is the risk that the investors' returns will be negative when they are first drawing money out of their investments. Variable risk is a related concept that emphasizes that when we prepare a plan, we do so assuming returns will be earned on a linear basis—for example, 4 percent each and every year—but in reality, returns vary every year, even though they may average out to 4 percent. In the accumulation stages of your life, this varying return doesn't matter as much once your portfolio is sizeable but it does when you are in your withdrawal stage.

Let's look at the following example: Mary invests $100,000 in a balanced mutual fund that earns the following over the next 10 years: 17%, 8%, -5%, 11%, -2%, 12%, 5%, 13%, -6%, -8%. The value of Mary's investment after the 10 years is $150,066. Because Mary is not taking any money out of her investments (or adding to them), it doesn't matter what order her returns appear in—the end result will be a value of $150,066. So if her returns actually panned out in the opposite order (-8%, -6%, 13%, 5%, 12%, -2%, 11%, -5%, 8%, 17%), she'd still have $150,066.

But it's a different story if Mary is withdrawing money from her investment. In our first example, Mary would see her $100,000 increase to $106,930 if she took out $4,000 at the end of each year to live off. If the sequence of returns were the exact opposite, however, she would see her capital decrease to $95,519. This is a difference of about $11,000 (almost three payments) after only 10 years, and the result could possibly be more dramatic if the portfolio declines were more significant like those that were experienced in 2008.

The point to understand here is that negative investment returns will affect you a lot more seriously when you are in the retirement stage than the previous two stages, particularly in the early years of drawing income. You will need to evaluate your income sources each year and not just follow some schedule that was linearly established in a plan.

Math versus Reality

Often our planning decisions are based on "the math," that is, based on mathematical calculations and projections using past data and linear estimates (once again, a fancy way of saying that everything from savings to withdrawals to investment returns will happen evenly).

But life doesn't happen that way. Sometimes we don't get the investment returns we were hoping to earn even if we haven't done anything wrong in our investment approach. Sometimes we don't truly understand our emotional DNA, and we end up being too aggressive or too conservative. Sometimes we make mistakes. And sometimes we incur unforeseen expenditures, such as needing to help a child out with some substantial money if he or she is going through difficult times.

All strategies and investment products have good and bad things about them, which can minimize some issues that arise and can make others worse. When you decide on the appropriate strategy or strategies (you can adopt more than one) for your retirement savings, consider what flexibility it offers you to change should you decide to do so and how well it will help you to sleep at night, and then try to strike a balance between meeting your emotional and lifestyle needs.

Investor Behaviour and Experience

If you have not had a lifetime of making investment decisions, you may find having to manage your portfolio an overwhelming task. A study conducted by Dalbar Inc. in 2005 showed that investors make wrong decisions an overwhelming percent of the time during down markets, and investors earn significantly lower returns than market averages or professionally managed portfolios because of investor behaviour.

Your investment experience and tolerance for handling volatility will have a bearing on the types of strategies that you can feel comfortable with.

Your Income Sources

You may have a variety of different income sources in retirement. There are the Canada and Quebec Pension Plan and Old Age Security payments for those who qualify, and you may have a company pension plan and perhaps a survivor's pension. If you've followed the BAPKIN Plan, you should also have savings that you've built up in your TFSA, RRSPs, and investment accounts to provide for any shortfall in income. You may also have income from part-time work for part of your retirement.

Some of these sources will provide guaranteed income and inflation protection, while others will not. Persons with company pensions may find themselves having a higher risk tolerance for their investments since they have more guaranteed income.

Your Cash Flow Requirements

There are three financial objectives that retirees have: you will need to cover your essential living expenses, you'll want to cover your desired lifestyle expenses, and you may also want to provide an estate for your loved ones. Unfortunately, there are other expenses that may arise, such as helping family members or dealing with a crisis that can't necessarily be planned for.

Many people are tempted to spend more in the early years of their retirement because they have better health, are more active, and have felt like they have put off doing the things they've wanted to do for too long. However, it's best to ease into a spending pattern so that you don't deplete your capital too quickly. Once you get a feel for your basic and modest lifestyle expense needs, then you can adjust your lifestyle expenditures accordingly.

Tax Considerations

You will want to earn income in a way that results in the least amount of taxes for your required level of lifestyle and that prevents clawbacks of social benefits and tax credits. Because you are emphasizing income over growth at this stage of your life, taxes can have a more meaningful effect on the strategy that you are following.

The general concept is to get income from the least tax-efficient income sources in your lower tax brackets and to use more tax-efficient income sources to round out your desired income levels.

Inflation

Rising costs are a fact of life. There may be a few times throughout history when overall prices of goods and services were falling but for the most part the trend is for our costs of living to increase. Investors often fail to factor in the effect of inflation on their lifestyle and estate plans.

The strategies and investment products that you make use of should address inflation, or you should at least see the effects that inflation can have on your lifestyle and financial objectives before you commit to any long-term strategy.

Outliving Your Savings

There are many reasons why you might outlive your savings: spending too much, earning too little on your investments, living too long (if there is such a thing), rising costs of living, and perhaps expensive health issues particularly later in life.

Besides working longer or on a part-time basis, shortfalls can also be eased by cutting back your planned spending or downsizing to a smaller home.

Be aware that this is a real concern and stress-test your strategies to see if they'll hold up against these issues.

Survivor Considerations

If you are presently married or living common law, you should think about what will happen to your income sources and expenditures when you or your spouse passes away during retirement. For example, you would only get one Old Age Security amount; you may receive a survivor Canada Pension Plan, but it won't fully compensate you for the loss of your spouse's CPP, and your spouse's company pension typically falls to 60 or 70 percent of what it was paying while he or she was alive.

You may also find that yours and your spouse's combined RRIF accounts now pay out a minimum payment that puts the survivor into a higher tax bracket and subject to OAS clawback. Other factors may come into play too such as the investment experience and knowledge of the surviving spouse. Recognize that the strategy may need to change in such an event.

Products: The Good, the Bad, and the Funky

Key investment products for the retirement stage:

As the saying goes, there are many ways to skin a cat, and so too there are many investment products that are suited for persons who require income in the retirement stage. Here is a list of some of these investments, including that which is considered good (G) and bad (B) about the investment product.

Guaranteed Investment Certificates (GICs). Most everyone knows what a GIC is. GICs with banks are protected by the Canada Deposit Insurance Corporation to the tune of $100,000 per "account," per institution, so you may want to spread out your investments if you have significant capital. It's convenient if you use an adviser who has access to different institution's GICs. If you were going to use GICs, a laddered approach is a good technique to adopt, which we will address in Step 8: "Beyond the Napkin—Have a Disciplined Investment Strategy."

The BAPKIN Plan

- (G) The value of a GIC does not deviate for statement purposes, so you don't get scared when you see the monthly statements.
- (G) You know in advance the rate of return that you are going to earn.
- (G) There is a significant amount of deposit insurance protection if you spread out your holdings.
- (B) You need to do some legwork and overall strategizing if you spread out your holdings amongst various institutions if you aren't using an adviser.
- (B) There is no tax efficiency. Interest income is taxed at your highest marginal tax rate.
- (B) Interest rates are low at this time and GICs seldom keep pace with inflation and taxes.
- (B) Most GICs must be held to maturity, thereby limiting your ability to take advantage of opportunities.

Insurance companies also have their version of GICs, sometimes called GIAs (Guaranteed Investment Annuity), which usually offer competitive yields but have the advantage of a named beneficiary, which then lets the investment be paid out to your beneficiary should you pass away, without having to go through probate. This would be an effective investment in non-registered accounts.

Recently, banks have been issuing GICs that have returns linked to a basket of securities. While these are good for offering potential returns better than GIC interest rates, you also run the risk of earning substantially less. Be sure to review the details of how returns are calculated and check out the good and bad comments for Principal Protected Notes (below), which are similar and just as funky.

Government Bonds. Government bonds, be they Government of Canada or provincial, are guaranteed by the respective government issuer, who has taxing power over its citizens. Bonds can also be used in a laddered approach and can have longer-term maturities than GICs.

- (G) You know in advance the rate of return that you are going to earn if you hold the bond to maturity.
- (G) Bonds can be sold prior to their maturity.

- (G) There is the potential for capital appreciation if interest rates fall below the yield you buy the bond at and you sell it prior to its maturity.
- (G) If you were to buy a bond at a discount to its maturity value, the difference that you receive between your purchase price and the value you receive at maturity will be a capital gain in non-registered accounts.
- (G) Maturities can be as long as 30 years.
- (G) Government of Canada bonds are considered the safest fixed income investment, and there is no restriction to the amount of dollars that are protected.
- (B) Bond interest rates are low at this time and may be lower than GICs.
- (B) It can be very hard to find bonds that trade at a discount during periods of low interest rates, and bonds bought at a premium are not tax friendly.
- (B) Bond prices fluctuate up and down based on interest rate movements, and these price changes can sometimes be significant. The portfolio value on your statement can decline so be prepared to see your portfolio value shrink due to bond pricing.

Corporate bonds are similar to government bonds, except their guarantee only lies in the issuer's ability to repay. They are therefore higher risk and so typically have higher yields associated with them.

Segregated Mutual Funds. Segregated funds are mutual fund investments that are offered by insurance companies. They provide a principal guarantee for part of your capital if held for 10 years in return for you paying a higher management fee. However, though a principal guarantee may give you peace of mind, it should be kept in perspective. There have been very few periods in history where the market value of a diversified portfolio was lower than the cost after a 10-year period. There are even fewer periods where the market value is lower than 75 percent of the cost, which is what many of these funds now only provide protection for.

- (G) Principal or part of the principal is guaranteed at the end of a 10-year period.
- (G) Principal or part of the principal is protected in the event of your death.
- (G) Beneficiaries are designated, which allows the investments to avoid probate.
- (G) May provide creditor protection for registered and non-registered assets.
- (G) Can invest in a balanced allocation.
- (G) Can reset the guarantee if willing to hold for 10 more years upon reset.
- (B) Some firms only offer a principal protection of 75 percent upon a 10-year period.
- (B) Management expense ratios are higher than regular mutual funds and reduce overall returns.
- (B) Principal guarantee is negatively affected if the money is withdrawn before the 10-year anniversary.

There are also now segregated funds for estate preservation purposes, which provide better maturity and death benefit guarantees, but they are not intended to provide income.

Tax-Class Mutual Funds. A tax-class mutual fund is a mutual fund with the objective of paying out income efficiently to unit holders. The fund typically pays out a set percent such as 5 or 8 percent, based on the value of the portfolio at the start of the year or at the time of your investment. The amount is sometimes reset at the beginning of each year depending on the fund.

- (G) Monthly income is usually paid based on the fund's net asset value at a period of time, such as the beginning of the year, and is known in advance one year at a time.
- (G) Most of the cash flow is paid as a return of capital, thereby deferring income tax until a later period.
- (G) Many popular mutual funds offer tax-class versions, allowing you more comfort in choosing managers and brands that you are familiar with.
- (G) Returns can be earned consistent with a balanced portfolio.

- (B) There is no guarantee for a return of your capital.
- (B) If markets decline, the payout might be reduced to preserve capital, leaving you short of required income.
- (B) If the mutual fund is held for a significant period, there could be a sizeable capital gain to be reported when finally sold.

Some mutual fund companies also offer Corporate Class mutual funds, which can defer some of the capital gains taxes.

Principal Protected Notes. Principal protected notes are debt instruments that, as a minimum, guarantee the return of capital to the investor after a given time, usually between 5 to 10 years. They provide returns linked to a basket of securities.

- (G) One hundred percent of principal is guaranteed upon maturity of the note.
- (G) There is some limited marketability to the note.
- (G) Returns can be significantly higher than fixed income investments.
- (B) The formulas for how your return is going to be determined are complex and difficult to estimate, and your returns can end up being lower than fixed income investments of a comparable maturity.
- (B) The return provided to you does not include the dividends earned on the securities, which can represent as much as half the return on the market over the long term.
- (B) Returns are typically capped (e.g., at 10 percent).
- (B) Income earned is taxed as interest income rather than capital gain and thus is not tax efficient.

Annuities. An annuity is an insurance product that pays you a monthly income for a set period. The most common annuity is a life annuity, which pays you income for life. The amount of income you receive is based on your age, the capital you are committing, your health, and current interest rates.

- (G) You know in advance the minimum monthly income that will be received.
- (G) The annuity can be indexed for inflation.

- (G) The annuity typically pays a higher guaranteed income than other investments.
- (G) Once an annuity is established, no further decision making is required from you.
- (G) It can be somewhat tax-efficient if the annuity is prescribed and funds used are outside of a registered account.
- (B) Payments typically stop upon death and no money pays into your estate unless there is a minimum guarantee remaining.
- (B) There is no accessing capital for other needs once the annuity is established.
- (B) Any guaranteed minimum payout reduces the monthly amount you receive.

Variable Annuities. These are also known as *Guaranteed Lifetime Withdrawal Benefit (GLWB)* investments and are available with insurance companies. With a variable annuity, your capital is invested in mutual funds. At a given age, you are guaranteed a minimum monthly income.

- (G) If your investments earn greater than the minimum being guaranteed, then the level of income you receive goes up each reset period.
- (G) You know in advance the minimum level of income you are going to be receiving throughout the guarantee period, which could be for life.
- (G) The program insulates you from any losses that might be incurred on the portfolio in the early years of your retirement.
- (G) You have access to your capital should you need it.
- (G) Bonus income amounts are paid for every year you do not withdraw any income from the investment.
- (G) Your beneficiaries get the remaining value of the portfolio upon your death.
- (B) There may not be a remaining value of the portfolio upon your death.
- (B) Taking additional capital out of the program diminishes the amount of the minimum guarantee.

- (B) Management expense ratios are higher than regular mutual funds and reduce overall returns.
- (B) Minimum guarantees are mostly the return of your invested capital over a lengthy period.

Insured Annuities. An insured annuity is achieved by combining two insurance company products: a permanent insurance policy and a prescribed annuity. Insured annuities are good for people who want the guaranteed income of an annuity but also want to preserve their capital for their heirs.

- (G) Prescribed annuities receive preferential tax treatment so the insured annuity provides a higher after-tax return than GICs.
- (G) You know in advance how much cash flow you will be receiving each month.
- (G) It can be done on a single or a joint-life basis.
- (G) You receive income for life.
- (G) Your estate receives the insurance proceeds tax free and avoiding probate.
- (B) If interest rates are low when you invest in the annuity, you will be locking into a lower payment for life.
- (B) You have to be insurable and that's not a done deal when you are older.
- (B) There's no accessing your capital after you've committed to the annuity.

Preferred Shares. Preferred shares are hybrid investments that have characteristics of both bonds and stocks. There are different features of preferred shares: some have fixed yields while others are fixed and then have rates that float with government bond rates. Some have dividends that accumulate if not paid, and others are not cumulative. Most preferred shares are perpetual in term, with clauses that allow the company to redeem them for a set price at any time after a given date. Some have a retractable feature that allows the investor to sell the shares back to the company at a given price and at a given time if the investor wishes to do so. Preferred shareholders do not have a vote on corporate matters and don't share in the growth of the business.

- (G) Dividends received are subject to preferential tax treatment if the issuer is a Canadian company.
- (G) Should the company go bankrupt, preferred shareholders rank before common shareholders for settlement purposes, and dividends must be paid to preferred shareholders before dividends can be paid to common shareholders.
- (G) Dividend income is known at the time of investment and is usually fixed until redemption. Yields on preferred shares are usually higher than long-term bond yields.
- (G) Preferred shares trade on stock exchanges and there is potential for capital gains if the shares are bought at a price below where they are redeemed or sold for on the open market.
- (B) Preferred shares trade on stock exchanges and there is possible capital loss if the shares are bought at a price above where they are redeemed or sold for on the open market.
- (B) While it is not desirable for a company to stop paying preferred share dividends, if dividends are halted there is no means of forcing the company into bankruptcy or forcing the company to pay the dividends going forward.
- (B) Preferred shares can be fairly illiquid in their trading, and this can have a profound effect on their volatility and on the portfolio values that show up on statements.
- (B) Though dividends receive preferential tax treatment, they may have a negative impact on tax credits and clawbacks.

Dividend-Paying Common Shares. The largest, most stable businesses typically pay dividends on their common shares. These dividends are not guaranteed to be paid, but many businesses with stable incomes have policies of paying a percentage of the profits out to shareholders. Companies that pay consistent dividends are very hesitant to reduce the amount that they pay per share, even when their earnings deteriorate.

- (G) Dividends received are subject to preferential tax treatment if the issuer is a Canadian company.
- (G) Dividends can grow over time if the earnings of the company grow.
- (G) Shareholders can enjoy the benefits of both rising dividends (income) and rising share prices (capital gains) when a company's business is doing well.
- (B) Dividends do not have to be paid by a company and shareholders cannot force a company into bankruptcy if dividends aren't paid.
- (B) If a company reduces its dividend payments, the share price usually declines by a significant amount.
- (B) Though dividends receive preferential tax treatment they may have a negative impact on tax credits and clawbacks.
- (B) Common share prices can be volatile and companies can go bankrupt, with serious negative consequences to the shareholders.

> **What's an ex-dividend date?**
>
> The ex-dividend date is the date a stock trades without a buyer being entitled to receive the current declared dividend. If all things remained equal, the share price should fall by the dividend being paid per share on the ex-dividend date. I often observe the price to fall the day after the ex-dividend date rather than the day of and have long wondered whether that was due to some investors' misunderstanding of the terms.
>
> Regardless, whether you are buying or selling a common or preferred share, pay attention to its ex-dividend date.

These were some of the more common investments that investors looking for income in the retirement stage make use of. It's good to have an understanding of the benefits and problems of each type of investment that you invest in. It's also good to understand the objectives and issues that your investments are supposed to address. Nothing is perfect. What matters is that it's appropriate.

Retirement Projections

What should a retirement income projection look like? Figures 7-1 (B) to 7-4 (B) show the type of information that a projection will have. Note how the information is presented with an adjustment for inflation so that you can better understand what sort of lifestyle your capital may provide based on your life experience now.

There are several factors that go into a retirement planning projection, but two of the most important are (1) the rate of return that you are planning on earning and (2) your retirement age. The rate of return you will earn should be driven by your risk tolerance and not by your "need" to earn a certain return. You will have no control over how investments will perform in the longer term. If you're falling short of your plan, your retirement date is sometimes the only factor that you have control over that will make a significant change.

> 👍 **THUMBPRINT**
>
> Have a Retirement Income Projection determined for you based on conservative investment return expectations and factoring in inflation. Ask your adviser to show it to you in terms of both annual cash flow and monthly cash flow, since people comprehend differently when seeing it in both perspectives. Remember, the math is just the math and may not represent what exactly is going to occur, but at least you can gain general impressions as to whether you're in good shape or up the creek and can then do something about it.

Pre-tax Retirement Projection

Assumptions:	RSP			Pension		Other Income		Non-Registered	
Current age	54	Yield to retirement	3.50%	CPP	$ 11,500	Other income	$ 12,000	Current non-registered	$ 30,000
Current RRSP	$ 350,000	Yield at retirement	3.50%	CPP age	65	Age starting	65	Annual savings	$ 5,000
RSP contributions	$ -			OAS	$ 6,300	Age ending	70	Capital depleted by	95
Retirement age	65			Pension	$ 8,868			Non-reg yield to retirement	3.50%
RRSP depletion starts	65	Inflation	2.50%	Age to start	65			Non-reg yield at retirement	3.50%
RRSP depleted by	95	Current year	2011	Index at retire	0.00%				

Year	Age	Apprx. End of Year Balance RRSP	Non-regstrd	RRSP Income	Non-regstrd Income	CPP	OAS	Pension	Other Income	Total Income	Capital Drawdown	Total Cashflow	Current Dollars
2011	54	$ 362,250	$ 31,050	$ -	$ -	$ -	$ -	$ -	$ -	$ -	$ -	$ -	$ -
2012	55	374,929	37,312										
2013	56	388,051	43,793										
2014	57	401,633	50,500										
2015	58	415,690	57,443										
2016	59	430,239	64,628										
2017	60	445,298	72,065										
2018	61	460,883	79,763										
2019	62	477,014	87,729										
2020	63	493,710	95,975										
2021	64	510,989	104,509										
2022	65	509,213	104,145	18,996	3,585	15,089	8,266	8,868	12,000	67,104	363	67,467	51,420
2023	66	506,883	103,669	19,471	3,982	15,466	8,473	8,868	12,000	68,260	477	68,737	51,110
2024	67	503,968	103,073	19,958	4,082	15,853	8,685	8,868	12,000	69,445	596	70,041	50,809
2025	68	500,434	102,350	20,457	4,184	16,249	8,902	8,868	12,000	70,659	723	71,382	50,519
2026	69	496,248	101,494	20,968	4,288	16,655	9,124	8,868	12,000	71,904	856	72,760	50,239
2027	70	491,372	100,497	21,492	4,395	17,072	9,352	8,868	12,000	73,180	997	74,177	49,968
2028	71	485,770	99,351	22,029	4,505	17,499	9,586	8,868	-	62,488	1,146	63,634	41,820
2029	72	479,401	98,048	22,580	4,618	17,936	9,826	8,868	-	63,828	1,303	65,131	41,760

Source: WealthTrust

Figure 7-1 (B)—*a schedule of various income sources. Note the "Current Dollars" column adjusts the cash flow for the effects of inflation so that it shows what that amount would be like if you were spending it today.*

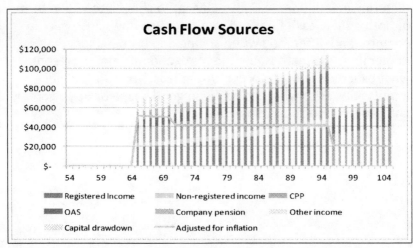

Source: WealthTrust

Figure 7-2 (B)—*demonstrates the cash flow in annual format. Note the inflation-adjusted estimate of the annual cash flow.*

The BAPKIN Plan

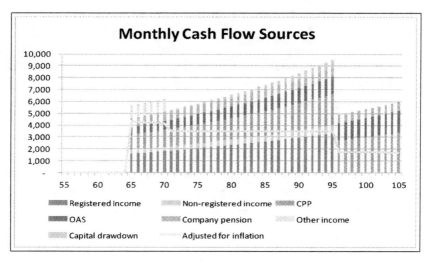

Source: WealthTrust

Figure 7-3 (B)—*demonstrates the cash flow from a monthly perspective. Note the inflation-adjusted estimate of the monthly cash flow.*

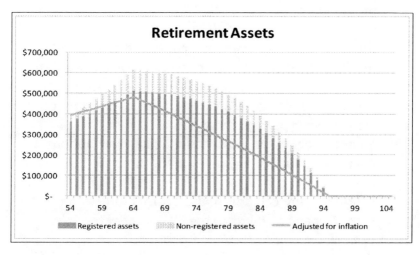

Source: WealthTrust

Figure 7-4 (B)—*demonstrates the capital balance remaining per period. Note the inflation-adjusted value that your heirs would be receiving.*

Individual Pension Plans (for Business Owners, Executives, and Incorporated Professionals)

Owners of incorporated businesses, their families, key executives, and incorporated professionals can establish registered, defined-benefit pension plans—similar to those enjoyed by teachers and government workers—known as Individual Pension Plans.

The ideal candidate is one of the above identified persons who is older than 40 years of age and who earns more than $128,000. Because an IPP is a longer-term contractual obligation, the businesses should be well established and generate consistent annual profits.

The key benefits of an IPP:

- You will be provided with predetermined retirement benefits—in other words, you'll know at retirement how much pension money you are able to receive each year, and you can even include features, such as inflation protection.
- More money is allowed to be contributed to your retirement account each year compared to an RRSP—as much as 65 percent more, so you can have much greater savings and any pension surplus will belong to you.
- You and your company can contribute for past service to increase your pension amount.
- Your company can make additional contributions to make up for up for any investment shortfalls below 7.5 percent.
- Your company can contribute up to 120 days after its fiscal year end rather than the 60 days after the calendar year allowed for an RRSP contribution.
- Your plan assets are likely subject to full creditor proofing.
- Your company can make a significant tax-deductible contribution at your retirement.
- You can split your pension for income tax purposes as soon as you retire and you can fund a survivor pension for your spouse.

- Your company can deduct the IPP administration expenses.

Ah, but we know there are always negatives to anything we may do. What are the IPP's biggest drawbacks?

- It costs money to set up and annually administer an IPP—it's usually about $3,000 to $5,000 to set up, and then there are ongoing fees, such as actuarial costs, throughout the life of the plan.
- Your company must make annual contributions, regardless of whether it has fallen on hard times.
- Your plan assets are locked up until you retire, unlike an RRSP, which you can always access.
- It is not as flexible as an RRSP from an investment perspective. The allowed investments are more conservative than RRSP eligibility rules.

It is worth exploring the IPP option with your adviser if you qualify for such a vehicle; however, you need to be aware of both the positive and the negative consequences of establishing such a plan.

STEP 8: BEYOND THE NAPKIN—HAVE A DISCIPLINED INVESTMENT STRATEGY

Some of the more detailed Beyond the Napkin strategies are next. We'll start off with a little bit of fun to set the table and then dig into the meat and potatoes with a detailed primer on investments, investment strategies, behavioural issues, and performance measurement.

Being information gluttons, dessert will be served in "Part III: Dessert," where I've included academic and professional investment influences and a framework for making financial decisions. *Bon appétit!*

An Imaginary Conversation: What Types of Investments Are Out There?

In the words of Monty Python, "And now for something completely different."

I have spoken with quite a few people recently who seem to provide a good cross-section of the types of interests that people are currently experiencing. Had I met them all at the same time and carried on one conversation about investments, the conversation may have gone something like this:

I'm sitting in an iconic Canadian coffee shop—let's call it "The Hortons"—and I'm talking with several distinct characters. Pete

Pessimist is the guy who never stays invested long enough in any particular asset class to make it worthwhile. He shows up late to the party and leaves late. He's got the investment world's equivalent of ADD. He feels he never makes any money and thinks that advisers are guys "in the know" about speculative investments and inside information.

Rhonda Realestate is in love with bricks and mortar. Rumour has it that she sleeps on it in the way that Scrooge McDuck liked sleeping on a mattress with his money hidden in it. To her, nothing else even stands a chance in investment worthiness. Her boyfriends more than likely have chiselled chests and hearts of stone to match.

Karen Tiffany loves the shiny stuff. Whether it is diamonds, gold, or a guy with black oily hair, she's into it.

Keith Kranium is a simple fellow, simple as in village idiot and he knows little about investing.

I would get the ball rolling by saying, "Let's start by looking at the main classes of investments out there. There are many types of investments available for most investors. The main classifications are cash, fixed income, equities, commodities, and real estate. Within these broad categories are a multitude of individual investments, mutual funds, closed end funds, and ..."

I can see Pete looking at me with wide eyes.

"Relax, Pete. Most of us just focus on the first three. Some people are adamant that real estate is the greatest wealth builder, but let's just say that though I think owning your own home is a fabulous investment, I wouldn't go out of my way to be a landlord."

Rhonda lets out a small cough and mumbles something like "bush it," but I just ignore her.

"What about commodities?" Karen asks. "Hasn't gold been rising significantly in the last few years?"

"I'll touch on gold in a minute. Not too many people open up commodity accounts anymore. Heck, all the major brokerages got rid of their retail commodity guys years ago. Too much risk. It was like having a bit of the Wild West as part of the territory that you had to sheriff. Besides, not too many people understand wheat, corn, zinc, or molybdenum, and even fewer want to actually own the physical product. I guess some guys will buy a physical commodity, such as gold coins, but, well, those guys usually wear tinfoil hats. Most people now own commodity-type investments by owning shares of companies that are commodity producers, but we would normally classify this from an asset allocation perspective as owning equities rather than commodities.

"Okay, so it's obvious that I'm somewhat biased because I've already got a passion for equities. I love them. I believe in them. I think them to be the best asset class for the majority of investors to be involved with, provided that you have a long enough time frame."

Pete's shaking his head. "I don't know. I think Florida real estate's looking pretty good right now."

"US estate taxes aside, maybe it is, especially with the Canadian dollar as high as it is at this time. But what's not to love about equities? Equities kick butt when it comes to the amount of investment returns they provide over long periods. Equities kick butt when it comes to outpacing inflation. Income earned from stocks is tax efficient, meaning it's taxed at a lower rate than other forms of income that can be earned. And equities are liquid. They are one of the most easily bought and sold form of investment that you can own—and with a very reasonable rate of commission, I might add."

Now Rhonda's rolling her eyes. "C'mon. You're the guy always preaching that salespeople (oh, that stung) never do enough to tell you the downside of an investment. We all know that you can lose a lot of money owning stocks. They can't be all that wonderful."

I answer her carefully. "Better returns, better inflation protection, better taxation, better marketability. C'mon Rhonda, what's not to like? But yes, alas, equities do have their weaknesses. The main one is that everything that is 'better' about stocks is better in the long run, not necessarily in the short term, and you have to be psychologically equipped to invest in them because of their gyrations."

"How long do you mean by 'long run'?" quips Keith. "I just turned 50. I don't even want to buy green bananas anymore."

"Let's just say we're looking at least five years. Ten years plus is more practical. In one of my lectures, I showed my students how the performance of various indices has been over one-, five-, and ten-year rolling periods. Look at these three charts. When you see how few, the number of times negative total returns occur over longer periods, such as five and ten years, and when you introduce a judgment about the reasonableness of current valuations, you get to be more comfortable with the asset class."

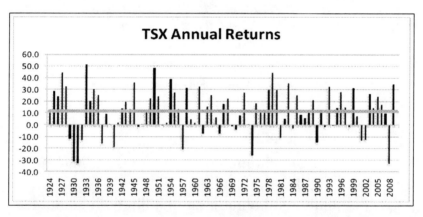

Source: WealthTrust

Figure 8-1 (B) *Negative returns have occurred about 25 percent of the time on an annual basis since 1924.*

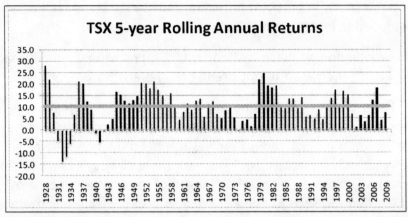

Figure 8-2 (B) *Negative 5-year average returns only occurred in 8 out of the 81 rolling 5-year periods. So if you bought and held for five years, you would have had negative returns only eight times since 1924.*

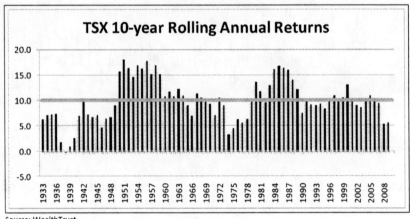

Figure 8-3 (B) *Negative 10-year average returns only occurred once in over 76 rolling 10-year periods. So, though you may have been ticked off if you lost money over that one 10-year period, is it really worth avoiding the asset class altogether considering its more typical performance?*

Rhonda wasn't letting go. "I'm sure there's more negative stuff than that?"

"Yes. Another weakness is that you have to either know what you are doing when investing in equities, or entrust your money to someone else who does. But hey, is this any different from real estate? This even goes if you are going to make use of exchange traded funds, known as ETFs to us acronym lovers, representing the indices. You will need to have patience. You will need to understand how the markets work, as well as the process of investing, and you will need to be disciplined about it."

"So where does the psychology stuff come in?" Keith asks, contemplating when his next medication is due.

"Emotional and behavioural aspects can easily shake you out of a proven investment strategy. We all have behavioural demons. The Fidelity Magellan Fund was one of the most successful mutual funds in the United States, yet Fidelity had reported that only a fraction of its investors saw the returns that the fund generated, because investors frequently bought and sold the fund, usually at inopportune times. Investors used to hold their mutual fund investments an average of about 12 years in the 1960s and 1970s. Now investors hold their investments approximately three years.

"The investment research firm, Dalbar, periodically does a study on returns achieved on the S&P500 index, the average equity fund manager, and the average retail investor. It comes up with similar results to the Fidelity findings. One that I saw a few years back, in 2006, showed a 20-year annualized return on the index of about 13 percent, but the average individual investor managed a lousy 4 percent."

"I'm that guy," shouts Pete, "and all that is due to what you call the 'behavioural demons' of the average investor?"

"Yepper, Petah. Man, I love Dickens's pronunciation. You will be deluged with media reports and well-meaning friends and advisers who will steer you in different directions. They aren't necessarily wrong directions, just *different* directions, and those different directions can result in you changing your strategy at, once again, inopportune times. Why? Because you are most likely to listen to them when you feel your strategy isn't working. You will be weak. You will be craving for someone to tell you that what you are doing is okay. It's human nature. But they won't tell you that. Instead they will steer you to a different investment class, or a different strategy or style of investing, or something.

"You will therefore leave a proven philosophy that hasn't been working for the last while. I mean, it could have been underperforming for several years, but perhaps it is on the cusp of being effective again. Instead you will move into another strategy or investment, which has been successful in the last few years and is just on the cusp of not working anymore. Thus you jump at the wrong time. What works is staying disciplined in the strategy you find meets your risk tolerance. Even better, employ several different strategies that complement each other, and stick to them. In the end, your character, discipline, and investment acumen will either help you or hurt you."

Pete breathes out an audible sigh, knowing very well from his years of watching *Buffy the Vampire Slayer* that fighting demons is all easier said than done. "Is *that* all there is to it then?" he says in a sarcastic tone.

"The final weakness with equities that I can think of right now is their variability of returns. It's real easy to say that stocks had a 9 percent average return in the last 10 years, but it's not so easy to stay invested when you start off making 2 percent, then lose 14 percent, and don't know that a 35 percent gain is right around the corner. Or how would you feel if you lost 10 percent first and then only made 2 percent, and then lost another 3 percent? Would you be hanging around to get that 9 percent average? Not likely. And yet it's what you are going to have to do in order to get those better returns."

"What can we do to try to stay invested? I, for one, would be irate if after three years of investing, I had less than when I started," Pete blurts out, likely saying what the others are thinking.

I stop to gather my thoughts. A quick look around outside The Horton's shows that the usual crowd of unique characters were busy going about their business in downtown Hamilton.

"Well, for starters, you can take comfort in knowing you have a balanced portfolio so that while the more volatile elements of your portfolio, namely your equities, are misbehaving, the other elements are protecting some of your capital. If you are earning dividend income, you can focus on the dividends you are receiving rather than on the value of your portfolio going up and down. Companies are usually hesitant to reduce dividends, and therefore the dividends tend to provide support to the share price.

"There are other things that you can do, and we'll touch on them another time, but I think the best thing you can do for yourself is to learn to stick with quality, understand valuation, and then focus on measuring your performance against an appropriate benchmark over longer periods, at least five years but preferably longer."

With that we get ourselves some more tea and coffee so that the good people at The Hortons wouldn't call mall security on us again.

Long-Run Advantages of Stocks

After we get settled back down I pass out a chart (Figure 8-4 (B)). Being too cheap to make several copies, I put it in the middle of the table for all to see either right side up or upside down. I chuckle as I remembered Bob Chan in grade-13 physics, straight off the boat from Hong Kong, reading the physics textbook upside down the day before our first exam. I think he got a higher mark than I did.

"I've already mentioned that over the long run, stocks have outperformed all other investment classes, yes, even including gold. Figure 8-4 (B) shows the long-term *real return* performance of various asset classes in Canada since 1949. 'Real return' means that it is adjusted for inflation.

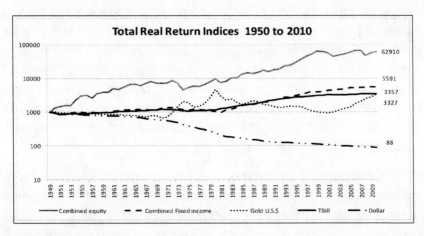

Figure 8-4 (B)—*total* real *returns of various asset classes: 1950 to December 2010.*

"You can see that stocks have vastly outperformed all other classes. Real estate isn't included in there, but I'll get to that in a bit. I won't go into details with the numbers, but by looking at the slope of the lines, you can see if the investment is increasing in real terms or merely keeping up with inflation over various periods of time."

I point to the various lines. "Stocks are the class with the greatest upward sloping line."

"Hold on here. Can you run this by me a little slower?" Keith looks a little perplexed.

"Okay. Look at the final values on the right side of the chart. The top line is a combined portfolio of the Canadian and US markets in terms of Canadian dollars. You can see that the fixed income index, which is a combined portfolio of bonds and GICs, has outperformed treasury bills and gold. The dollar has done the worst. Of course, what a dollar will buy you becomes less over time, and that is evident in the chart. That's what happens in an inflationary environment which is the normal type of environment that we live in. Prices to buy things rise over time, and thus the value of a dollar hiding in a mattress somewhere goes down—unless it becomes a collector's item for some reason. Deflationary periods are few and far between.

"It's interesting to see that gold, the investment bastion of 'ancient' advisers and conspiracy theorists the world over, does serve as an inflation hedge over the long run, but that is about all it had done in US dollar terms, right up until 2003. It didn't grow; it just kept its value. It is evident from the chart, however, that stocks can appreciate during inflationary periods."

"So what's the deal with gold being the 'hedge against inflation' rather than equities?" Karen asked.

"I don't really think it necessarily is, Karen. Remember the movie *Schindler's List,* when Schindler is 'buying' the workers and he opens up a briefcase to show a case full of Reich marks? At the end of the war those Reich marks lost about 80 percent of their value, and when the deutsche mark was introduced in 1948, it was at the rate of 10 Reich marks to one deutsche mark. The currency was worth very little but a case full of gold would have kept its value, because gold is an alternate currency."

Karen jumped in, "So, if you are expecting the world monetary system to crumble, or at least the monetary system where you work and get paid, gold may not be a bad thing."

"Yes. Whether it is crumbling because of hyperinflation, like what was experienced in Latin America in the 1980s, or the termination of the country as you know it because of war, it would be much better to own gold than to hold paper currency."

Stocks versus Real Estate

"Let's get back to Pete and Rhonda's current interest, real estate.

"Yes. I understand that you can't live in your portfolio, but you can live in a house. Yes, I do believe that owning a home should be a priority over owning an investment portfolio. And I do understand that with real estate, it is location, location, location. Hey, anybody remember that Peter Wong guy from those infomercials back in the 1980s, who used to preach on how to buy real estate with no money down using advances from a multitude of credit cards as the down payment? Ha, that was sweet. If by sweet I mean stupid. Where is that guy now?

"Sorry. I digress. Okay, I know that you could be charging rent on an investment property and making income although I will add that the income, net of expenses, would be fully taxed at your marginal rate.

"My example isn't going to be fair to someone who could have bought, say, in Toronto or New York or some other rapidly growing centre. Now that those have been said, let's look at the comparison of owning real estate in general rather than stocks as an investment.

"I know that in the past I've seen information stating that says that real estate keeps pace with inflation. Realize that this is in the long run. If inflation rears its head, then the central bankers raise interest rates in order to slow the economy. Increased interest rates makes real estate, which is typically bought highly leveraged, more expensive to carry and thus, in the short run, real estate prices are likely to fall, not increase, when inflation takes root.

"Whether or not you want to believe this, let's just look at an example on the comparison of real estate and stocks, where I have some firsthand experience.

"Let's say that you had $10,000 to invest at the start of 1955. You could have bought a house in a brand new subdivision in Hamilton, where they were tearing down vineyards to build these new homes. Hamilton was known as the 'industrious' city and was booming in the day. It even had a bee as its mascot to show just how busy it was.

"Rather than the investment properties, you also could have invested $10,000 in the Templeton Growth Fund. I chose this fund because it began its existence in November of 1954, so the dates are close.

"Fast forward into the year 2010, where Canadian real estate prices are booming and the world's stock markets are recovering after enduring two of the nastiest bear markets in the last 100 years. World markets in Canadian dollars were down about 50 percent before starting to recover in the fall of 2003 and were down 50 percent again in 2008. Despite that, you would see that the Templeton Growth Fund investment was worth about $5 million. The home was worth about $250,000, and net rents reinvested at 5 percent would have amounted to about $650,000. That would put the rental house worth about $900,000. Hmmm, $5 million versus $1 million?"

Rhonda was getting a little agitated. "You're probably low-balling that reinvestment rate."

"Yes, I know that the rental income could have been reinvested at a rate a bit higher than 5 percent over the long haul, although bonds have averaged just over 6 percent over that time frame, but I also know that there were rent controls in place since the 1970s, taxes had to be paid on the net rental income, there may have been times when the property was vacant, repairs needed to be done to maintain the property, and I haven't factored in any of these negatives in my calculations. I think I was being quite fair in my $650,000 income estimate. Besides the financial implications, a person would also have had the overall inconvenience of being a landlord, and I know that real estate is much less liquid than stocks—these are the two so-called PITA, or pain-in-the-ass, factors about real estate.

"You would have paid a fee to the Templeton organization to manage the money on your behalf," I said. "But that's already been factored in, and the tax you would have to pay on the capital gains on the fund is significantly lower than the tax on rental income. Besides, capital gains were tax free on the gains incurred up to 1972, when capital gains became taxable. At that point the capital gain on the Templeton Growth fund was greater than the gain on the house. Just to complicate my blurb, there was another capital gain shelter in 1994, when the tax laws changed yet again.

"The point to this is not to slam owning real estate but to show that equities have demonstrated themselves to be one of, if not, the best asset class to own for investors with a long-term time frame."

"Well," said Peter, "you've certainly given us a lot to think about. So are you saying that we should just be in stocks, then?"

"Not at all, Pete." I looked around and made sure I made eye contact with every one of them. It was tough to do with Rhonda due to the glare—as in the way she was glaring at me.

"Each of us needs to invest based on our risk tolerances and our financial objectives. And for almost all of us that involves being involved in all the main investment categories. Heck, Jacob Fugger the Rich told us way back in the fifteenth or sixteenth century to split our money up between bonds, stocks, real estate, and 'gold'—which in Jacob's day was 'cash.' That hasn't changed.

"What I'm saying is don't let what happened in the last 10 years determine whether you own stocks. There is just too much good about them to be afraid of them or ignore them completely. You just have to understand them better—that's all."

With that, we finished off our drinks, rolled up our cup rims—Rhonda won a coffee, which seemed to cheer her up—and said our good-byes.

End scenario.

Ah, that was fun. But while it's nice to say equities are oh-so-good, let's look at *why* they are such an attractive long-term investment:

Equities are living beings with long lives. Management and shareholders come and go, but the entity itself remains intact. If the company has a maturing or outdated product, such as buggy whips, management can change the focus of the business and have it do something different, but even if it doesn't, an investor can change the company he invests in very quickly and efficiently. He can also diversify more easily and in a more complete manner.

In high inflationary times stocks get hammered, but so do all other investments, except maybe gold. But the businesses can raise prices to cover some of their higher costs and can do things to lower their costs, such as replacing old inefficient equipment with new more efficient equipment in order to try to get back their profit margins and trudge ahead in value.

The market, as a whole collection of stocks, can grow along with the growth of the country. Some stocks may go bankrupt and some new stocks may emerge, but, collectively, business grows with the growth of a nation, and thus the mechanics are in place for stocks to appreciate over time.

Rah rah rah. I know. I don't really mean to promote equities as much as I've just done over the other asset classes, but given the bear market of 2008–2009, investors have become so shy of equities that a transfusion seems to be in order to provide new life to the asset mix conversation.

Fixed Income Primer

Every balanced portfolio will have fixed income investments, but many investors are not aware of the wide array of fixed income products that exist. We have already touched on the advantages and disadvantages of several fixed income investments, such as GICs and bonds in Beyond the Napkin Step 7, "Have a Personal Pension Plan Strategy," but here's another perspective of some of the more common fixed income investments that your adviser might be recommending. They are listed here to provide a quick synopsis if your adviser is recommending something you don't really understand.

Cash and "Near-Cash" Investments

Canada Savings Bonds/Provincial Savings Bonds
- Yields are comparable to short-term fixed income investments.
- Only available for purchase at certain times of the year.
- Can redeem at par only at certain times of the year.
- There's no price volatility on your monthly statement.

High-interest daily savings accounts
- Offer attractive short-term yields.
- Can be bought and sold anytime.
- Subject to $100,000 limit CDIC insurance protection.
- Interest is calculated daily and paid monthly.

- Interest rates change up or down based on short-term interest rates.
- May have a nominal cost to buy or sell.
- There's no price volatility on your monthly statement.

Money market mutual funds
- Similar to high-interest daily savings accounts, but do not have $100,000 CDIC protection and offer lower interest rates.

Fixed Income Investments

Guaranteed Investment Certificates (GICs)
- Not liquid, principal repaid at maturity or upon death or with a penalty if it's a "cashable" GIC.
- $100,000 limit on CDIC protection.
- Bought at par and priced at par so there's no volatility on your monthly statement.
- Most GIC maturities range from months to five years.

Government or Corporate Strip Bonds
- Provide compound growth and safety but no cash flow until maturity.
- You will have to pay tax on interest accrued each year, despite not receiving interest until maturity, if the bond is held in a taxable account.
- Priced at an estimated market value, so it will show volatility on your monthly statement.
- Capable of providing capital gains or losses in addition to accrued interest if sold prior to maturity. Pricing may not be as good as you expect, especially if you are selling smaller quantities.

Government of Canada or Provincial Bonds
- Interest is tax-disadvantaged but paid periodically, usually semiannually.
- If bought at a discount to par then part of the return will be taxed as a capital gain rather than interest.

- It can be difficult to find discount-priced bonds when interest rates are low.
- If bought at a premium to par then tax disadvantaged in a taxable account, since higher coupon interest is taxed at your marginal tax rate, but the loss at maturity is treated as a capital loss and only deductible against capital gains, which are taxed at a lower rate to begin with.
- Priced at estimated market value so it will show volatility on your monthly statement.
- Capable of providing capital gains or losses if sold prior to maturity, but pricing may not be as good as you expect, especially if you are selling smaller quantities.

Real Return Bonds

- Government bonds pay an interest rate relative to the actual inflation rate over the life of the bond.
- They are not very liquid and all existing maturities are long term, so it should be bought and held for long periods.
- The capital invested appreciates by the inflation factor thereby maintaining the purchasing power of the bond over its life.
- The capital appreciation that occurs on the principal due to the inflation factor is taxed as ordinary income as it accrues each year, even though you don't receive the income until the bond matures.
- Priced at estimated market value so it will show volatility on your monthly statement.

Corporate Bonds

- Interest income is tax disadvantaged.
- Credit quality does matter and can improve or deteriorate while you hold the bond.
- Most corporate bonds can be called by the issuing company prior to maturity.
- Diversification is a necessity for protection when investing in lower grade issues.

- Yields can be higher than government bonds, but it's important to evaluate spreads, because sometimes they are only marginally better.
- Capable of providing capital gains or losses in addition to accrued interest if sold prior to maturity.
- Priced at estimated market value, so it will show volatility on your monthly statement.

Preferred Shares

- Dividends are tax advantaged.
- Those that offer a safety net (i.e., a retraction feature) are priced higher and yield less.
- Those that offer resets at favourable terms are priced higher and are more likely to be called than reset.
- Often difficult to acquire large positions in the market due to limited liquidity.
- Shares can be redeemed at the company's request.
- Capable of providing capital gains or losses if sold prior to maturity.
- Priced at market value and limited liquidity so it will show volatility on your monthly statement.

Floating Rate Bonds and Preferred Shares

- The characteristics for these securities are similar to the characteristics of bonds and preferred shares, except that the interest rate or dividend yield usually starts out at a fixed rate. Then, after a period of time, for example five years, it becomes a rate that floats with a benchmark rate, such as the Bank of Canada rate.

Principal Protected Notes and Security-Linked GICs

- Returns are linked to the price action on a basket of securities, there are usually limitations to the maximum return that can be earned, you don't get the dividends earned on the basket of securities, and most often there is a convoluted means of determining what rate of return is earned.
- Must usually wait for maturity to receive interest income which is undeterminable until that time.

- In times of serious market deterioration, a safety mechanism is invoked so then there is no potential to recover market losses and provide a return before the maturity.
- Principal is usually guaranteed.
- Might have limited marketability.
- Income is treated as interest income so is tax disadvantaged.
- No price volatility on your monthly statement.

> **Liquidity versus Marketability**
>
> Is there a difference? Yes, there is. Any investment that can be sold is marketable. The question is, "At what price?" Investments that trade with a small price spread between the buyers and sellers, and with lots of volume, are liquid. If they trade with wider spreads and/or there is hardly any quantity available to be bought, or hardly any buyers who want to buy when you are selling, these investments are illiquid and will be more costly to trade, since you will likely get a lousy price for what you are doing.

Of course, there are fixed income mutual funds and exchange-traded funds that invest in many of the above noted investments. Though they'll charge a fee, or you'll have to pay a commission to invest in them, they provide excellent liquidity to the investor, which often cannot be obtained by holding the individual security, and this can be a very important investment objective. The important thing to note is that most fixed income investments are marketable and will therefore fluctuate on your statements each month.

It's also important to note that any normal fixed income investment with a maturity date will provide you with a return that is known in advance if you hold the investment to maturity, but if the investment does not have a maturity, such as a bond mutual fund or a perpetual preferred share, then the long-term return will likely approximate where current interest rates are around the time of your investment—but there are no guarantees. For some, a maturity date is a very valuable emotional feature.

There's also a few other things that you should understand before we start talking about fixed income strategies.

1. *Short- and long-term interest rates.* There is a difference between how the two are determined. Several theories explain why rates are set the way they are, but in short, long-term interest rates are influenced mostly by investors' perception of inflation. That's because the investors lock into a rate of return for a long period, and rising inflation can ravage the purchasing power of their return and capital. Short-term interest rates, on the other hand, are influenced by many different things, including government policy decisions, the attempt to influence the economy and inflation by a country's central bank, and even foreign currency issues.

    So when we think about long-term interest rates, we think mostly about inflation when trying to predict if the rates will go up or down.

2. *Taxation.* Interest income earned on bonds is taxed at your highest marginal tax rate meaning it's taxed just like your employment income, so there's no tax advantage to be had from the interest you receive. However, most people buy bonds from their financial institution's inventory or the secondary market and not upon new issue, so it's likely that the bond will be trading either above (a premium) or below (a discount) its par or maturity value.

> 👍 **THUMBPRINT**
>
> Whenever possible, buy bonds at a discount in taxable accounts. Buying bonds priced at a premium in a taxable account has negative tax consequences, since you are paying your highest tax rate on the interest you receive but then the money you lose at maturity is only benefitting you by one half of your tax rate, at best.
>
> Think you've outsmarted everyone by buying compound strip bonds that don't pay interest until their maturity in your taxable account? Nice try. Interest that accrues must be brought into income each year, so now you have to come up with the cash to pay the tax—but you haven't received any interest yet.

If you hold the bond to maturity, the premium that you paid above par will be treated as a capital loss at that time. If you bought at a discount, you will receive more money than what you paid for the bond, and this will be treated as a capital gain. Of course, if you do this in a registered account the point is moot, but if done in a non-registered account, then only one half of the gain or loss is brought into income. As with all capital losses, they can only be applied against capital gains and not deducted against any other form of income.

3. *Yield curve.* This is another important concept for investors to understand. The yield curve is a visual representation of federal government interest rate yields for each given period of maturity, as can be seen in the two charts (Figure 8-5 (B)). A normal yield curve is one where shorter-term interest rates carry a lower yield than those fixed income investments with longer-term maturities. If shorter-term interest rates are higher than long-term interest rates, this is known as an inverted yield curve, and it is the bond market's omen that a recession may be forthcoming. Remember, a recession is bad for equities, so this is one of our warning signals for our tactical component to possibly reduce our exposure.

In Figure 8-5 (B), the chart on the left, both the Canadian and US yield curves have normal slopes. This suggests that bullish economic conditions are in place. The Canadian yields are higher than the US ones over shorter maturities, but at about 10 years the yields are comparable, and then the US bonds offer higher returns.

The chart on the right shows the Canadian yield curve over three different time periods—December 14, 2010, one month previous to that, and one year before. You can see from the chart that current yields from maturity terms of 5 years onward are higher than where they were one month previous but lower than where they were a year ago. You can also see the steepness of the curve over the short-term maturities (from 1 to 10 years) and then the flattening of the increase in rates after 10 years.

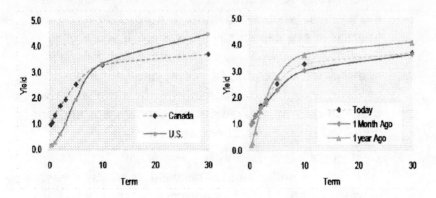

Source: Raymond James Ltd.

Figure 8-5 (B) Example of yield curves (as at December 14, 2010).

Investors can use the yield curve to determine how much they are being compensated for investing in other fixed income investments relative to government bonds, and they can also use it as an indicator of overall economic conditions.

4. *Other considerations.* Bond prices and investors' returns are affected by interest rate changes, as well as the length

of maturity, the coupon rate, and the credit quality of the bond investment.
- All things being equal, the longer the time until the bond matures, the more volatile the bond price will be when reacting to changes in interest rates and credit quality.
- All things being equal, the higher the interest coupon rate of the bond, the lower the volatility of the bond when reacting to changes in interest rates and credit quality.

A bond's market value is like a teeter-totter. The price of the bond moves up and down in the opposite direction of the movement of interest rates. Thus when interest rates decline, the price of the bond rises and significant capital appreciation can be generated. The longer the term of the bond, the bigger the price moves.

Another thing to remember is that, as implied above, the lesser the interest coupon, the bigger the price move will be. Thus, zero coupon (or strip bonds) will have bigger price moves up and down than a bond with a 3 percent interest coupon. And the 3 percent interest coupon bond will have bigger price moves up and down than a bond with a 6 percent coupon.

Let's look at some examples:

(a) A 30-year bond with a 4 percent coupon is issued at par when interest rates are 4 percent. That bond will be worth $1,000 when issued. If interest rates were to rise to 6 percent the very next day, the value of the bond would fall to $723; if rates were to fall to 3 percent, the value of the bond would increase to almost $1,200. Here you can see how the bond price moves opposite the changes in the market interest rate.

(b) Let's now say that another 30-year bond is issued at the same time, that is when rates are 4 percent, but this one has no coupon. It is a compound bond, also called a zero-coupon or a strip bond. Because there are no interest payments until maturity, the bond would be issued at about $305 and will mature at $1,000 in 30 years' time. If rates were to rise to 6 percent, the bond would only be worth $170. That's a decline of 44 percent, whereas the bond in example (a) only fell 28 percent when rates had risen. But it works to the investor's favour if rates were to fall. If rates were to fall to 3 percent, the bond would appreciate to $409—a stunning 34 percent increase in price versus the increase of 20 percent in example (a).

You can see how the "coupon" you are receiving each period affects the price changes in the bonds, and just how sizeable those gains or losses can be. Imagine if you had bought $50,000 worth of the strip bond rather than $305!

> 👍 **THUMBPRINT**
>
> In periods of rising interest rates, it is best to be invested in a basket of short-term fixed income investments such as 1- to 5-year laddered bonds or GICs, short-term bond funds, or short-term bond exchange traded funds. In periods of falling interest rates, it's best to be invested in long-term bonds, bond ETFs, or bond funds.

> 👍 **THUMBPRINT**
>
> It's tough to outperform bond indices because fees erode much of the extra gains made by managing a bond portfolio; however, value can be added if your portfolio manager or adviser makes use of duration management and corporate and provincial bonds. It's important to be properly diversified if investing in corporate bonds, particularly lower grade bonds. Duration management is a fancy way of saying switching your bond positions between long- and short-term maturities to take advantage of interest rate movements.

Fixed Income Investment Strategies (The Devil's in the Details)

Let's take a more detailed look at the fixed income strategies we can employ to get the most out of our fixed income investments. After all, going to the bank and deciding on an ad hoc basis what term of GIC we want isn't necessarily the most tax-efficient or best performing means of getting income. It should be noted also that all strategies can be used with each other by professionals, and they usually are.

The Ladder

The ladder is a technique where you split your fixed income capital evenly among different periods—most people do it for 1 to 5 years, but this isn't cast in stone. I've made use of longer ladders that encompass 10-year time frames, and even more.

But most people use 1 to 5 years, because that is the common maturity terms of guaranteed investment certificates that the banks offer, so for the rest of this discussion, I'll just assume that we're talking about a 5-year ladder.

The beauty of the ladder is that it eliminates the need to predict where interest rates are headed. You are simply resigning yourself to getting an average rate.

But the ladder also provides three other benefits. Recall what a normal yield curve looks like, where shorter-term interest rates are lower than longer-term interest rates. When following the ladder technique, each time a bond or GIC matures, you would reinvest the principal in a 5-year bond or GIC regardless of where you think interest rates are headed. The 5-year GIC normally has a higher interest rate than the other periods, so over time your portfolio will be earning the *average 5-year* rate rather than the lower yields.

Another benefit is having an element of liquidity. Because you've staggered your maturities, you will always have 20 percent of your fixed income capital coming due within one year. Of course, if you're making use of bonds rather than GICs, you could always sell them prior to maturity, and that would give you much better liquidity.

There is also comfort in knowing that a laddered fixed income portfolio does not need to be subject to the vagaries of market value fluctuations, since the investments all have maturity dates. If rates go up, just wait until the bond or GIC matures, and then you can reinvest at the new, higher rates.

One negative with a 1- to 5-year laddered approach is that there is very little additional return that can be earned since the maturities are short term in nature. Remember, the longer the term to maturity the more volatile the price and volatility can be a good thing when it means that the price is moving up.

The Barbell

The barbell is a Jekyll-and-Hyde approach to fixed income investing. It involves splitting up a portion of your fixed income capital to fixed income products that have short-term maturities and to fixed income products with long-term maturities. So, if you made use of two bonds, say, a 2-year and a 10-year, your fixed income portfolio would look like the weights on a barbell.

The purpose of the barbell is to have part of your capital (the shorter-term allocation) subject to less risk of price movement changes while the longer-term portion lets you earn higher yields.

There's no hard and fast rule on how you employ the barbell. It does not have to be equally weighted. It is merely a balancing tool for trying to achieve different investment objectives and handle risk management. You can allocate two thirds of your capital to the short-term portion and one third to the long-term portion. It all depends on what you are trying to achieve—safety, liquidity, income, capital gains, maximizing return, or perhaps the ability to lock in at higher yields if interest rates are climbing.

Think fixed income investments aren't risky?

Think again. There are many risks that fixed income products can expose you to such as:

- *Repayment and credit risk.* Even GICs can have this one. Maybe the company, government, or bank goes bankrupt and you'll have to wait to recoup some or all of your investment, or perhaps its financial condition deteriorates, which affects the price of your investment that you didn't plan on holding until its maturity.
- *Interest rate and yield curve risk.* Rates change continually and so will your bond or preferred share price.
- *Reinvestment risk.* You might find yourself reinvesting interest or dividend payments and matured or redeemed investments at lower and lower rates.
- *Liquidity risk.* You may need to get out but can't until maturity or maybe the price you get when you sell will be lousy because hardly anyone is out there who wants to buy.
- *Volatility risk.* Some fixed income investments are more volatile than others.
- *Event risk.* Remember the world financial system almost imploding in 2008?
- *Exchange rate risk.* Foreign bonds are subject to changes in currency values.
- And the greatest risk of all with fixed income products— loss of your purchasing power or *Inflation risk.*

You can even make use of laddered securities within your barbell. You might find that your adviser wants you to allocate part of your portfolio to a 1- to 5-year ladder of GICs and another part to a ladder of 20- to 25-year bonds.

Gerard Hass

Duration Management

I've already demonstrated how fixed income investments move up and down in price depending on interest rate movements and other variables, such as the coupon or dividend payments and the term until maturity.

Imagine if we had a crystal ball in which we were excellent at predicting where interest rates were heading. In year 2000, a 30-year government bond is yielding 5.64 percent. There's a negative yield curve in effect, but the long end of the curve is flat, with 10-year bonds yielding an attractive 5.52 percent.

We anticipate that interest rates are going to fall so we invest $100,000 into a new issue 5.64 percent coupon 30-year bond. To make the math simple, we'll assume that the bond pays interest annually, even though most bonds pay interest semi-annually. Of course, we have no intention of holding the bond for 30 years. We want to try to maximize our return, so we are going to hold for 10 years and then sell it because our crystal ball tells us that interest rates are going to be increasing again.

Fast forward 10 years and our 30-year bond has now become a 20-year bond. We have earned interest at 5.64 percent for the past 10 years, so we have received $5,640 per year. If we had bought the 10-year bond instead back in 2000, we would be receiving our principal back now, and we would have been earning $5,520 per year over this same time frame, so it's been nice to be getting a little extra yield. But wait— interest rates have fallen, and a 20-year bond now yields 3.95 percent, so what is our bond worth? Our 20-year bond, which we can sell, is now worth about $123,000. Scores! That means we earned an extra $23,000 by locking into a longer maturity.

Since we expect interest rates to increase in the forthcoming year, we sell the bond and allocate the $123,000 to a 2-year bond yielding 3.15 percent and will collect the interest until the longer-term rates climb back up, at which time we will sell and lock in to a longer-term maturity again.

This has been an example of duration management—the buying and selling of fixed income investments of differing maturities in order to take advantage of interest rate movements. A Canadian study done back at the turn of the millennium found duration management to be the best way to beat the fixed income indices. Of course, nobody has that crystal ball but most active professional bond managers make use of duration management to provide additional return to their clients.

Corporate and Provincial Bonds

Although this is not a strategy per se, the same study found that making greater use of corporate and provincial bonds also aided in outperforming the bond universe index. But you shouldn't just do this blindly. Often the yields on corporate and provincial bond issues are barely above the yields you get on government of Canada bonds, so make sure you are being adequately compensated for assuming a greater risk of repayment. The yield curve is the tool that we use to compare the additional yield that we are receiving.

Corporate bonds in particular require care in selection and diversification is a very important risk-management tool. High-yield bonds have greater risk of repayment. Diversification is a must if you are making use of high-yield fixed income products. Mutual funds and exchange traded funds exist which invest in these investments from both an active and passive basis; however, due to their lack of liquidity, many managers have settled on a passive approach. Besides diversification, credit management is a very important aspect of trying to outperform bond indices.

Anything else I should consider?

Other bonds that warrant your attention are real return bonds, also known as inflation bonds. These bonds have a set coupon rate, which is lower than coupon rates on regular bonds, but the rate is based on the inflation-adjusted value of the bond. Thus, you will receive increasing interest payments over time linked to inflation, and the principle value of your investment also grows by the rate of inflation so that at maturity, your capital has kept pace with inflation.

But don't just invest blindly in them. There are times when you are not being adequately compensated and would be better off in a traditional or nominal bond. It's best to compare the real return of a longer-term nominal bond, such as a 10-year bond Corporate and provincial bonds, with the yield on a real return bond to see if the pricing is worth it. Real return bonds should be held for very long periods and are best bought in non-taxable accounts, such as RRSPs, since the inflation compensation (i.e., the increase in value of the principal amount due to the increase in inflation) is taxed as interest income each year, even though no compensation is received until the bond matures or is sold.

Most advisers follow a combined approach to fixed income investment management so at least now you should have some idea as to what they are trying to achieve. It is important to keep your costs low if investing passively and employ professional management for an active management approach. When I practice duration management, I prefer to use long and short-term bond funds and ETFs because they give me better liquidity than if I were to buy the individual bonds.

Equity Primer

Stocks are equities, and it is this component of your portfolio that has the potential to provide the greatest impact on your lifestyle, either good or bad. Stocks and stock-based investments such as mutual funds or exchange-traded funds will likely be the most volatile and most exciting component of your financial plan and investment portfolio, and it is for this reason that you must carefully understand what you or your adviser is doing.

Although Pete Pessimist would argue me on this, there is no quick and dirty get-rich approach to investing in stocks. There is no foolproof system that ensures positive returns will be earned or that outperformance will be achieved. Investing in equities involves as much creativity as it does math, and there's even an element of luck involved. Those of us who manage money professionally know that we do so without certainty, so if you see that guy on the business channel speaking matter-of-factly about a stock, recognize that it's "more show than know," or else that he's delusional about his capabilities.

While individual stocks by no means are certain to appreciate, why is it that we can be more certain that diversified markets will appreciate in the long term? After all, the market represents an aggregate of these individual companies, so it stands to reason that we should not really be that confident. I think the answer lies in the observation that the population and the economy grow over time, and since businesses as a whole profit from this growth, it's only natural that their value will follow suit.

Ah, but what if populations shrink? A country's aging population does have a detrimental effect on its stock markets and productivity, but fortunately, or perhaps unfortunately, if you subscribe to the theory that we are becoming overpopulated, the world itself continues to expand, and many businesses now have worldwide operations and sales, which compensate for the decline in domestic sales.

A market's appreciation can be linked to three factors: dividend yields, growth in earnings, and a "speculation" factor represented by changes in the multiple that investors are willing to pay for those earnings based on their expectations. If you buy into markets when those expectations are lower than what the growth actually proves to be, you'll likely fare quite well.

What makes a stock appreciate? In my younger years, whenever I'd ask my good friend and colleague Tod why a stock was going up on a particular day, he would answer emphatically, "More buyers than sellers, Gerry." There you have it. That's why a stock price goes up: because there are more potential buyers than sellers, and inversely a stock will go down in price when there are more potential sellers than buyers. Shifts in supply and demand, an economist would call it.

The key to success when investing in stocks is to anticipate when there is going to be more buyers than sellers and to sell when you anticipate that there's going to be more sellers than buyers. I like to think of the investment world as one big Ponzi-pyramid of investors.

As long as people keep piling into the pyramid, the prices appreciate, but when they decide to sell, the pyramid inverts and prices drop.

So what are some of the reasons there will be more buyers than sellers? A stock represents ownership in a company, which operates a business. That business typically has sales and expenses, and its net profit allows it to pay dividends to the owners of its stock. If the company chooses not to pay all its profit in dividends, then it will reinvest its profit to generate even more sales, or it can buy back shares or reduce interest costs by paying down debt—all strategies designed to make even more profits. It is this cycle of revenue growth, cash flow growth, earnings growth, and dividend growth that gives a business its value.

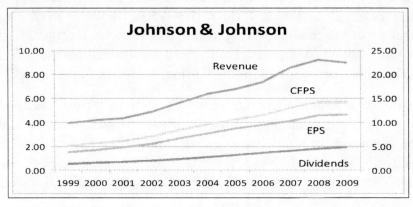

Source: WealthTrust

Figure 8-6 (B) *Ten-year summary of Johnson and Johnson that shows growing revenues per share, cash flow per share, earnings per share, and dividends per share (top to bottom). This type of profile is utopia for the buy-and-hold investor, but Canadian investors holding JNJ lost money throughout this period because of the appreciation of the Canadian dollar and the higher multiple (more than 30x in 1999) attributed to J&J's earnings, which has now fallen to about 15x.*

So if you are seeing a stock price rising, there will typically be an encouraging story related to it. It might be better earnings or sales being reported than the analysts forecast; it might be management increasing the dividend, it might be a new product coming to market or new management, the company's product's price rising in the case of commodities, or it can even be as general as interest rates falling, in which case all stocks look better because of a whole bunch of reasons. I like to think in terms of tailwinds and bottlenecks, and my strategies try to incorporate the two themes.

A tailwind pushes you forward rather than creating resistance, and tailwinds in the investment sense are happenings that make it easier for the price of your stock to appreciate. Real estate and the stock market, interest-sensitive stocks in particular, had a 30-year tailwind in the form of interest rates falling from 1982 to the present. Commodity stocks have had a tailwind for almost 10 years now, as China has been modernizing and requiring all forms of commodities to facilitate this modernization. Wealth management stocks have had a tailwind as baby boomers have been aging and building their wealth. Tailwinds tend to be longer term in nature.

Bottlenecks, on the other hand, are shorter term and represent shortages that may occur in the marketplace. Companies that provide the products or services where there are shortages are able to sell all that they can produce and are even able to raise their prices. Increasing prices and increasing volumes equal increasing sales which translate into higher earnings and dividends which of course is the cycle that helps the value of a business grow.

Investors who want to try and value a stock will forecast the growth they expect in the various business lines, taking into consideration these tailwinds and bottlenecks, and then will determine an intrinsic value for the stock. Intrinsic value is different from the actual stock price and is a fancy way of saying what we truly believe the stock to be worth. It can be estimated many different ways such as by discounting cash flows, applying a justified price-earnings multiple to the earnings per share, or even applying a dividend valuation model. We use all these techniques to rationally guesstimate the value of the stock. Based on our predictions, we will have an idea whether we feel the market is over-optimistic or over-pessimistic, and it helps us decide if we want to buy or sell the stock.

Fundamental, Quantitative, and Technical Analysis

So how is your money being managed? Most investment managers will follow at least one of the above titled techniques.

Fundamental analysis involves determining the estimated worth of a company and investing in those businesses that appear to be trading below their intrinsic value as I previously described. It can have excellent long-term results depending on the manager's forecasting skills. Buy-side research companies, such as Morningstar and Value Line, have demonstrated that portfolios built on their valuation methods have been successful in outperforming their benchmarks.

Quantitative analysis involves selecting a basket of stocks that have particular valuation or growth or momentum features, such as low price-to-earnings multiples or high quarterly earnings momentum, holding those stocks for a period, and then selling and selecting a new basket of stocks which meet the criteria. Quantitative analysis has excellent long-term performance results but was shown to have significant weaknesses when markets seriously deteriorate, as they did in 2008, because much of the criteria used in ranking the securities is based on historical data or analysts' estimates and changes to these estimates or data is not made fast enough. Still, the style can complement a fundamental approach, with the net result being smoother returns and better consistency for investors.

Technical analysis involves looking at stock charts and determining patterns and trends. Technical analysts believe that the pricing in the charts represents all that the market knows or feels at each point in time. Therefore, it is well suited to accommodate investor psychology. Examples of techniques that you can apply include using trend-lines and moving averages, and looking for formations such as head-and-shoulders, cups-with-handles, and double-bottoms. There are very few professional money managers that manage solely on a technical basis, but many incorporate the approach as part of their selection criteria. It's more likely to be used by an individual investor or a stockbroker as the main criteria for stock selection than it would with a professional money manager.

Technical analysis works best when there are distinctive trends, up or down, but can result in poor performance in sideway markets unless you correctly recognize the pattern. I've seen where technical signals on a security resulted in three small short-term losses, which combined to a total loss of 12 percent at year end, even though the security finished up 4 percent for the year had the investor just held without doing anything.

Passive versus Active Investing

Passive investing involves buying a basket of stocks, usually trying to emulate an index such as the S&P500, and then holding without making changes. Most exchange-traded funds apply a passive approach. Active investing involves buying securities based on fundamental, quantitative, or technical factors and making changes to the portfolio as the data changes. The goal of the active manager is to try and outperform the passive investment, after accounting for fees.

There is a continual debate over which approach is better. In large, well-researched markets such as in the United States, passive investing seems to have the upper hand in most rising or sideways markets, but active managers who are willing to carry significant cash balances can possibly do better than passive managers when markets are declining. Investors considering which approach they would find best should consider the volatility of the two approaches.

Remember the example I gave about the 200-day moving average line on the Dow Jones Industrial Average having a respectable return with a lot less volatility? Volatility is the enemy of many investors because it frightens them into making changes at inappropriate times so having an actively managed portfolio with less volatility may actually help them get better long-term returns than had they held passive investments and made changes out of fear or greed.

Many managers who are supposed to be active managers are actually "closet indexers," whereby their portfolios approximate the index against which they are measured, and they make only minor overweight or underweight allocations. The fees charged to manage the portfolio can mitigate any advantage that their judgments may have provided, and they often end up underperforming the index they are shadowing.

I think the capability for active managers to outperform depends on their investment approach. The Canadian market is one heavily weighted with resource and material stocks. Throughout the 1990s it was very easy to find managers who outperformed the TSX Composite Index, because most managers were value managers and very few value managers would buy resource and material stocks at that time because their earnings were inconsistent and their intrinsic value very hard to determine. This was fine for a decade, where these sectors went sideways at best.

But in the early-to-mid-"naughties" ('00s), energy and material stocks went ballistic and value-oriented active managers underperformed the index. Managers who were more resource-focussed or momentum-focussed fared better, and most of those outperformed because they significantly underweighted the other sectors, including the financial sector, which underperformed.

One could argue that if you had the ability to predict the correct style to invest with—value, growth, growth-at-a-reasonable-price, momentum, sector rotating, small cap, or large cap—an active manager and the investor would be very capable of outperforming the passive approach.

Investment Style

So can you predict the correct style to invest with? Unfortunately, as ideal as it seems, I know of no way to do this especially over shorter time frames.

Style Primer

Here's a quick rundown of the different styles that you might find appropriate:

Value. Value comes in many different forms. Value managers are looking for investments that trade below their intrinsic value using different value indicators, such as discounting cash flows and ratios. More popular ratios are price-to-cash flow, price-to-earnings, price-to-book, and price-to-sales. High dividend yields are also popular among value managers. Some value managers are deep discount managers—looking for stocks that trade at a very deep discount to what the manager feels they are worth—others use more of a quantitative approach, while others do so relative to the respective industry or the company's historical fundamentals.

Growth. Growth managers are looking for companies that demonstrate high sales growth and earnings growth. Valuation often means very little to the pure growth manager, who likely feels there will be a "greater fool" out there—someone who believes the growth will continue even further and is willing to buy the stock off them when they determine to sell it.

Growth at a reasonable price. Managers who follow this approach look for sustainable, consistent earnings growth but aren't willing to overpay for the stock. They will include the stock in the portfolio if it can be bought at a reasonable price.

Momentum. Momentum managers are looking for companies that demonstrate above-average growth in sales, earnings, or even stock price.

Sector rotating. A sector rotator is a manager who over-weights and under-weights his positions in various sectors based on what he thinks the optimal sectors are going to be.

> *Size of market capitalization.* Managers may invest in larger capitalization stocks, such as blue-chip companies that are widely traded, or in small capitalization stocks, which are smaller-sized businesses. Smaller-sized businesses often have faster growth characteristics because their size allows more rapid expansion, and they may have deeper valuations because they have less coverage by analysts and less ownership by the big investment institutions. But they can also be higher risk when their growth slows down or when their fundamentals deteriorate.
>
> *Blend.* A manager who applies a blended approach is seeking to incorporate the different styles and market capitalizations to the maximum advantage of the investor.

I think a better approach is to include style diversification when you are determining your asset mix. You can make use of investments and portfolio managers that provide different styles, and you can tailor it to your own tolerance for risk. Remember, it's not just about how much money you make, it's also about how well you sleep while it's invested.

Domestic versus Foreign Investments

It's often pointed out that Canada only represents about 4 percent of the world in market capitalization. In other words, we're somewhat insignificant, and the rationale is that because of this, you should be investing in global securities in order to be better diversified and to open yourself to better opportunities.

Of course, anybody following this advice has had a bad taste for the past decade, as the Canadian market significantly outperformed many of the world's larger markets thanks to Canada's conservative banking and insurance rules and its abundance of natural resources.

Adding insult to injury, Canadian investors who made use of foreign investments, such as global equity mutual funds, were further punished by the appreciation of the Canadian dollar, which made their foreign investments worth less in terms of Canadian dollars. After a decade, many global indices were down around 25 to 40 percent in Canadian dollar terms. That's a lot to be down after sitting there for 10 years.

Some global equity managers had hedged the currency and their performance is substantially better and even positive, but most managers had not hedged currencies. There are now many more investment opportunities available that give you a choice between hedging and not hedging the investment, and this is one more consideration that you must make when determining the investments to invest in.

Of course, if I were writing this book a decade ago, quite opposite results would have been written. Back then the United States and global market investments boasted a decade of 15-plus percent returns, which put the Canadian market returns to shame, and currency devaluation was a big part of the outperformance. So don't let the more recent bias influence your thinking too heavily when deciding on the approach that's right for you. There will be more on that when we look at investors' behavioural issues. The simple approach of splitting your foreign investments fifty-fifty between hedged and unhedged positions may be best.

What's an Exchange-Traded Fund (ETF)?

One of the greatest ways to invest passively in domestic and foreign markets is by making use of exchange-traded funds. Exchange-traded funds are quickly growing in popularity for investors because they provide flexibility and diversification with costs significantly lower than actively managed mutual funds. So what is an ETF?

Most of us are familiar with mutual funds. Mutual funds are "open-ended," meaning that we can buy and sell each day at the net asset value of the portfolio as of the end of the day. Our monies flow directly to and from the portfolio with each transaction. The advantage of open-end mutual funds is that you receive the net asset value of what the investment is worth. There is no discount.

The problem is that you are getting the price at the close of the day, but you had to put your order in earlier in the day. Normally it's not a big deal, but imagine if you put your order in to sell your fund in the morning when the markets were up 1 percent, but during the day news came out that caused the market to sell off, and it ended up down 3 percent at the close. Having to wait for end-of-day pricing "cost" you 4 percent. It does happen, but not too often.

There are also "closed-end" mutual funds. These funds do not receive or pay out cash each day. Instead, they initially receive their cash to invest by issuing shares on the stock market and then go about their business managing the money in the portfolio. You want to invest in the fund or get your money back? Not the fund's problem—it's up to you to buy shares or sell the shares you own in the stock market, and you would pay a commission to do so each time, as you would any stock that trades on an exchange.

The advantage of closed-end funds is that you can sell or buy at market prices throughout the day without having to worry about end-of-day pricing. A typical problem with closed-end funds is liquidity. Unless there are many other investors who want to buy or sell the security, there tends to be a sizeable gap between the bid that someone is willing to pay (likely this is what you'll get if you want to sell) and the ask that someone wants to receive (this is typically what investors will pay if they really want to buy). I've seen these gaps be as large as 5 percent.

The closed-end fund is also usually actively managed, and the management fee can be as high as it is for an open-end mutual fund. They often only price their portfolio periodically, such as weekly, so much of the time you don't really know the true net asset value of what you are buying and selling.

Enter the exchange-traded fund. The exchange-traded fund operates similar to the closed-end fund, except it usually is not actively managed and it charges a low management fee because of that. Most of the ETFs out there represent an index or investment theme. For example, the Standard and Poor's 500 is a closely followed American index representing 500 of some of the largest corporations in the United States. But an index is not an investable security—it is a fictional basket of stocks with no fees and no trading costs—yet many investors find that they cannot outperform the index and would gladly receive a return which approximates it. So an ETF was established that invests in a basket of stocks designed to mirror the return of the S&P500, minus a low management fee. Voila, investors have an approximate way to invest in the index.

A big advantage of the more popular exchange-traded funds is their liquidity—they will typically trade one penny apart on the bid and ask, and most are priced every day, so you know what their net asset value approximates. They are available representing so many different markets, indices, and investment sectors. Some hedge foreign currencies, while others do not and they aren't just available for stocks. There are also ETFs that represent bond indices and inverse market returns, amongst other areas.

The list of ETFs is growing every year. With that growth come a few pitfalls. The more ETFs that become available representing similar investments, the greater the potential reduction in liquidity. Also, investors often blindly invest in ETFs without understanding what they are comprised of, but ETFs often don't provide as much diversification as you might believe and so need to be understood. For example, Nortel once represented 37 percent of the Canadian market. Imagine if you came into my office and I said to you, "I'm going to put about 40 percent of your money in one stock, and the rest we'll diversify around." You'd think I was crazy, yet this is often how some indices and ETFs are weighted. I remember Mexico at one point having three stocks representing almost half its index. You need to understand these risks and do some homework before you invest.

	Canada S&P / TSX60	U.S. S&P 500	Europe/ Asia MSCI EAFE	China, Brazil, India MSCI Emg Mkt
GIC Sector				
Financials	31%	15%	25%	25%
Energy	26%	11%	7%	14%
Materials	21%	4%	10%	14%
Telecommunication	5%	3%	6%	8%
Industrials	5%	10%	12%	7%
Consumer Discetionary	5%	10%	10%	7%
Consumer Staples	2%	11%	10%	7%
Information technology	2%	18%	5%	13%
Utilities	1%	4%	5%	3%
Health Care	1%	11%	9%	1%

Source: WealthTrust, January 2011

Know Your Market!

Figure 8-7 (A) *Indices have different sector weightings. Here are four of the more popular indices that investors can access through ETFs. Note how the Canadian market has almost 50 percent attributable to the Energy and Materials sectors, whereas the S&P500 has a more even distribution among its sectors. Note also the major geographic diversification that can be achieved in these four ETFs.*

	Percentage change as of December 31, 2010				Annualized return since
Style Portfolios	1 year	3 year	5 year	10 year	December 31, 1985
Bargain	26.1	-1.8	6.3	9.4	10.5
Earnings Value	15.4	13.4	19.7	22.1	17.7
Income	21.3	4.6	3.8	13.7	14.6
Predicatable Growth	7.9	-3.6	5.6	13.8	14.6
Momentum	5.1	-7.3	2.5	12.8	21.5
Dangerous	15.8	-5.8	-5.2	-12.6	-7.2
Index					
S&P/TSX Composite					
Total Return	17.6	2.1	6.5	6.6	9.0

Source: CPMS

Figure 8-7 (B) *Different styles can outperform indices over the long term. Here, several styles are shown to outperform over 10-year and 25-year time frames but not necessarily over 5-year time frames or shorter. Ever wonder what would happen if you went into bizarro world and did everything the opposite of what I'm telling you? The "dangerous" portfolio represents the outcome of such folly.*

Equity Investment Strategies (Size Matters)

Much of what you should be doing will depend on the size of your account. The principles of asset allocation, diversification, and rebalancing should dominate your strategy, and it takes a bit of money to properly follow those principles on a cost-effective basis if you plan on making use of individual stocks. So unless you have a significant amount of savings, mutual funds and exchange-traded funds are the most appropriate investment vehicles for your investment dollars.

If you do have savings built up of $100,000 or greater you can make use of cost-effective professional management, such as investing directly with a portfolio manager or investment counsellor, or you can invest on your own or through your broker and invest in securities directly rather than through a mutual fund.

Your strategy should be influenced by your objectives for your money and where you are in the life stage. Risk tolerance, financial objectives, time horizon, and investment experience are all factors in deciding what's right for you. Depending on your situation, it is sometimes more effective to make use of mutual funds that have tax advantages, such as T-Class mutual funds, or segregated funds that have capital guarantees, or S-Class mutual funds that pay a percent to you each month as cash flow rather than to own individual securities. It's a discussion worth having with your adviser.

As your savings build, here are some strategies that I follow that you and your adviser might employ.

Mutual Fund or ETF Portfolio

Investors with less than $100,000 can achieve great results by making use of mutual funds or exchange-traded funds. The traditional diversified portfolio invests in mutual funds and ETFs utilizing different investment styles, capitalizations, and geographic areas. For example, let's say you consider yourself to have moderate risk tolerance and were going to allocate $70,000 to equity investments. You might put $20,000 into broad-based global mutual funds—say $10,000 into two separate funds, one that hedges the dollar and one that doesn't—and the remaining $50,000 would be allocated to Canadian equity funds and ETFs—say $20,000 into a low-cost ETF that represents 60 of the largest Canadian companies; $10,000 into a growth-oriented fund that uses sales and earnings momentum to select its portfolio; $10,000 into a conservative mutual fund that will hold a lot of cash when it finds the market expensive; and $10,000 into a small-cap mutual fund.

There are many different combinations and permutations that you can create. The idea is to understand how the manager manages money or what the sector allocations and stock compositions are of the ETF and to go with what you are comfortable with, not just what has had good numbers in the past.

Core and Explore

A variation on the traditional theme is to go with a core portfolio of broad-based mutual funds or ETFs and to allocate a set dollar amount or percentage of assets with which to take greater risks with or to put into a specific market sector.

So in our example above, instead of investing in the denominations stated, perhaps we would invest 20 percent less into each fund and instead invest $4,000 each into three individual stocks and $2,000 into a particular sector ETF, such as gold.

We make use of a *core and explore* strategy when we want to own individual securities but don't have enough money to properly diversify, or if we are trying to outperform an index. There's more information about trying to outperform an index in Part III, "Dessert," of the book.

Integrated Style Portfolio

I strongly believe that investors are happiest when they earn positive absolute returns and when they know that part of their capital is being protected when markets deteriorate. While we can't always show positive absolute returns when investing in the stock market, we can try to protect capital and reduce volatility.

Since different styles do well at different times, why not try to reduce this volatility by combining styles and include a tactical component? Figure 8-8 (B) shows the results of three different management approaches—a value/yield style, a growth style, and a tactical component—and Figure 8-9 (B) shows the combined results of integrating these three approaches. The data in the figures includes a 2 percent management fee and has been back-tested to 1990. It demonstrates how style diversification and capital protection techniques can be effective tools to growing your wealth.

The value/yield style is comprised of stocks with the features of growing dividends and business fundamentals, reasonable valuations, and reasonable expectations for capital appreciation. The growth style emphasizes stocks with fundamental momentum (such as fast growing earnings and cash flows) and price momentum. The tactical component uses a simple monthly moving average, similar to how Jeremy Siegel tested to determine if the investor is in or out of the market for part of the portfolio.

Reviewing Figure 8-8 (B), it's interesting to note that the value/yield style had superior performance relative to the index right out the gate, but the growth strategy underperformed the index and the other approaches for seven years until 1997. The tactical component typically underperforms its index because of fees, until there is some sort of market meltdown, and then the tactical component shows its worth. The Canadian market saw two such meltdowns in the last 20 years—2001 to 2002 and 2008 to 2009.

Of the three approaches, the value/yield style was still the dominant approach until 2003 when energy and material stocks became the engines of growth for the Canadian market thanks to China and the emerging markets. The value/yield style reached its peak in 2005 and then it became a question of "what have you done for me lately" when its value declined from $1.2 million (from a $100,000 base in 1990) down to just more than $900,000 in 2009. Investors who came later to the party and put their money into that one style would not be too happy by 2010, despite the style's 12.3 percent 19-year return.

The growth style surpassed the value/yield style in total worth in 2006 and continued to appreciate even factoring in the 2008/09 market correction. Overall, its 19-year return is an impressive 14.5 percent after fees, and $100,000 fictitiously grew to $1.3 million by the end of 2009.

The tactical component underperformed all styles and the index for a decade. Many investors would say, "Why even bother?" but that's okay, because its job is to reduce the portfolio's volatility so you aren't scared out of the program. The tactical component rises from the ashes in 2001 when the market corrects thanks to Nortel's bubble being burst and never looks back, gaining even more ground on the index in the 2008 selloff.

The BAPKIN Plan

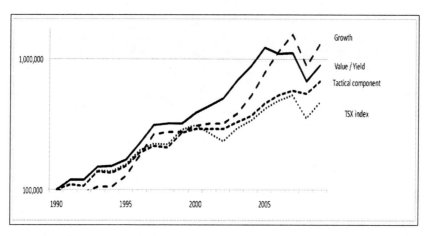

Source: WealthTrust

Figure 8-8 (B) *This chart demonstrates the performance of three distinct investment styles.*

Combining the portfolios into one portfolio starting at $100,000 and allocating 40 percent to the value/yield style; 20 percent to the growth style; and 40 percent to the tactical component shows appreciation to more than $940,000 in the 19-year period without any rebalancing (Figure 8-9 (B)). Note that the heavier weightings were allocated to the two styles that performed the least and that represent the more conservative styles of investing. This is just an example of how differing styles can complement each other.

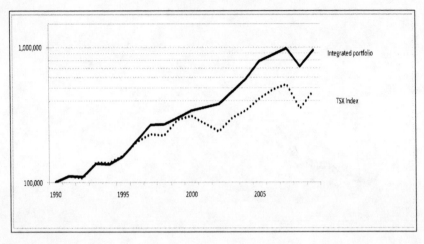

Source: WealthTrust

Figure 8-9 (B) *The chart above shows the lower volatility and better performance of combining a value/yield style with a growth style and including a tactical component.*

Understanding Investor Behaviour (We Really Are Our Own Worst Enemy)

You need to understand that there is a difference between market behaviour and investor behaviour. Market behaviour is the ups and downs of the market which is rational in the long run but can be very irrational in the short term. Investor behaviour is more personal, and it's how we react to the market's behaviour or to events that are occurring in our portfolio.

Unfortunately, the way investors are wired makes them act opposite to the way good investors act. When you go shopping and you see prices of quality items that you need on sale, you buy them and if it is a product that you use often, you will likely buy as much as you can.

When stocks go on sale, however, we get nervous that they are going to be worthless or are going to become cheaper, and so we panic and want to sell them. It's our nature, and it is the complete opposite response to what we should be doing. If we don't keep our emotions in check, we risk letting *our investor behaviour*, rather than the market's behaviour, affect our portfolio's performance.

Behavioural scientists have been examining our emotional wiring in order to get a better understanding as to why we think like we do when it comes to investing, and they have identified several behavioural issues that we need to address in order to remain successful, disciplined investors.

Unwitting tactician. We may consciously decide to employ a tactical component into our investment strategy, but often we do so unwittingly, with a detrimental effect on our return. How do we do that? When investors are faced with extreme volatility or a shortfall in performance, they sometimes stop their systematic savings or allocate their new savings to other asset classes that they perceive to be safer.

We can avoid becoming unwitting tacticians by ensuring that we don't stop our savings program and by forcing ourselves to rebalance our portfolio in accordance with how we decided rebalancing was to be done when we first decided on our strategy.

Framing. Framing is how we look at things or how things have been presented to us. If we are told that the market appreciated an average 10 percent for the past five years and our portfolio appreciated 4 percent, we may be disappointed at our results. Yet we may have invested more conservatively in dividend-paying stocks that did not appreciate compared to the more cyclical sectors of the market but were better suited to our objectives.

I think the greatest culprit to our developing framing issues, besides the use of selective hindsight, is selective advertising. Banks will display big banners in their branches of their best performing mutual funds, mutual fund companies will advertise only their best performing funds in newspapers, and advisers will show prospective clients sample portfolios built with the benefit of hindsight. These give us misleading perspectives as to how we should have been doing.

If we let ourselves be influenced by framing issues, we risk changing our strategy, even though it may have been better suited for our risk tolerances and objectives. We risk being that guy that continually changes to the faster lane on a gridlocked highway, only to get no further ahead but endangering himself and everyone else around him.

Anchoring. We often key in on a particular piece of data on which we then base future decisions even if the data isn't relevant to the decision we are making. For example, investors will often focus on the price they paid for a stock and won't sell unless they at least make their money back, whereas the decision to buy or sell is irrelevant to the price they paid. Just because you paid $20 for Bombardier in 2000 doesn't mean its price is going to go back there. The decision to buy more or sell should be based on where you think the price is going to go from where it is now.

I once had a client not sell a stock because he wanted to see it hit $10. The price was $9.90 at the time. The stock price never did hit $10 and eventually went bankrupt. He lost thousands of dollars because he anchored his decision to sell on a set price. Worse, I've known investors who refused to sell hundreds of thousands of dollars of Nortel because of the tax that would have to be paid. Now, that money has completely disappeared. I've also seen investors who will not buy back into an investment because the price is higher than what they sold it at. Again, this price is irrelevant, but investors' behaviour will stop them from reentering the market when it may be appropriate to do so.

In order to avoid anchoring issues, investors are best served by having decided upon a disciplined process and strategy and sticking to it.

Herding. We find safety and strength when part of a group. We are likely conditioned to this "not going against the crowd" from our caveman days in order to ensure self-preservation. After all, if we were different from the others, we find ourselves getting kicked out of the tribe or bonked on the head in the middle of the night.

We apply the same conditioning to our investments—we seek reinforcement from others that we are all doing the same thing.

But it might not be the right thing for you. Just because that guy on television took your call and told you that he really likes the stock you asked about and that it's in his portfolio doesn't mean it's the right thing to own. Just because friends at a party are discussing how much money they are making in technology stocks doesn't mean you should be investing in them.

More money is made by investing in stocks where the growth expected by the market is lower than what the growth actually pans out to be, and more money is lost when it is invested in stocks where the market is expecting much higher growth than what actually pans out. Herding keeps you from investing in the former and encourages you to invest in the latter.

While it's sometimes better to be a contrarian and go against the crowd, it is best to do so when you think the crowd is going to change their minds and follow you at some point—sooner rather than later. There's also nothing wrong with following a trend, if that's part of your investment strategy, but you need to recognize that you are part of a herd and that you will need a discipline on when to change your direction. The gazelles at the front of the pack don't get eaten. There's a lot to be said for independent thinking.

Loss aversion. Contrary to popular belief, investors aren't risk averse. Investors don't mind volatility if it comes in the form of stock prices rising substantially above normal price increases, and they don't mind taking on risk if they feel they'll be rewarded for it.

Instead, investors are loss averse. We detest losing, so much so that we appear to hate losing twice as much as we like winning. It must be absolute hell being a Toronto sports fan.

Because we hate losing, we may find ourselves selling out at market lows when others are also selling in great quantities, because we can't foresee anything that will make things get better and we just don't want to see any further losses. The result? We end up participating in the final blow-off. Investors who sold out at market lows in 2009 may have been suffering from loss aversion.

You should understand the negative implications of every investment you make. Every single investment has good and bad things about it. Understanding volatility and the risks that you can tolerate are the keys to you investing properly. A proper asset mix and proper diversification are necessary to address your aversion to losing money.

Recency bias. Bonds have appreciated throughout the decade thanks to declining interest rates. The Canadian stock market has been appreciating for the past seven years, but global equity mutual fund returns have been dismal. Guess where most investors want to invest their money?

Remember Newton's first law that an object in motion will remain in motion unless acted upon by an external force? Our thinking works the same way. We believe events that we see occurring will continue to occur. While it can be very profitable to follow a trend, we must be prepared to change our investment and our way of thinking when that trend is broken. It's a good idea to go back and reread the last paragraph of the section on herding if it hasn't sunk in yet.

Understanding why investments have risen or fallen in the past is a good basis for mitigating recency bias. Having a strategic asset mix and rebalancing are ways to keep recency bias in check.

Overconfidence. I remember a financial adviser in the mid-naughties sending out a recommendation to buy Alcan Aluminium on the basis that the world's airlines were going to be upgrading their fleets which would result in an increased demand for aluminium. The share price drifted downward for months after the recommendation was made but then rose dramatically on a takeover by Rio Tinto.

The adviser, happy of his recommendation's outcome, sent out a letter to his clients and prospects congratulating himself regarding his savvy advice. Yet the outcome had nothing to do with the rationale for his initial recommendation. He got lucky—that was all.

People tend to believe their skill level is much higher than it really is. If we aren't careful, we can get fooled by randomness and attribute positive outcomes to our skill rather than luck or a trend over which we had no control. It's been found that overconfidence can lead to excessive trading and often results in more aggressive investing than what the investor would normally be comfortable with.

Often investors will keep their savings in cash investments and withhold going into the market until they feel more confident. The result is that they come late to the party, investing late in a cycle after seeing several years of positive results. Of course, being late in the cycle they are often caught buying at the top of the market.

Once again, this behavioural issue can be minimized by sticking to a strategic allocation and rebalancing in order to minimize the overreaction that can occur with overconfidence.

These behavioural concepts are by no means exhaustive of the behavioural finance field, but I've included them in this book so you'll recognize the importance of following disciplines and investment concepts that you understand, so mental demons will not hurt your investment performance.

Performance Measurement (It All Comes Down to Perspective and Framing)

Think about this. You have an asset mix of 70 percent equity mutual funds and 30 percent fixed income, and things have been going very well. You've enjoyed a couple of years of good market returns, but now you're starting to get nervous about the markets. There's rumblings that interest rates are going to increase, there's debt problems in foreign countries, and you think that we might even head into a recession, so you're prudent and you reduce your equity weighting to 60 percent in March and then reduce it again before the summer so that you have an asset mix of 50 percent fixed income and 50 percent equity as you go into the summer.

You're happy with your tactical shifts because they met your risk tolerance levels, and you're happy that you employ a tactical component because you feel it's going to help you outperform. You make no further changes to the portfolio and come year end, you see that your portfolio appreciated 7 percent, and you hear on the radio that the "market" was up 14 percent. Happy?

How about this scenario? You like to buy individual stocks and believe that high dividend-paying stocks are the most appropriate for you, including companies in the United States. You like their conservative nature and don't mind that the majority of the stocks you own are pipeline companies, banks, insurance companies, health care businesses, and electrical utilities. Five years go by and you find the stock component of your portfolio is down 20 percent from its high. You do some digging and find that the stock market has risen 50 percent over this same time frame. What the heck? How could that be? After doing further research, you see that the market increase was due to appreciating energy and material stocks, of which you owned hardly any because they didn't pay safe or large enough dividends, and that the Canadian dollar appreciated, hurting your American holdings. Happy?

I think that often it is our perception of how we are doing and how we *should* be doing that influences our desire to stick to an investment strategy. Friends at parties will brag and tell their fish tales that make themselves appear smart and make you feel like you're missing the boat; the media will report market performance that isn't relevant to your asset mix, risk tolerance, or strategy; and seldom does anyone factor hidden values that you may be receiving, such as tax savings and estate efficiency, into your evaluation.

I remember a client once putting his neighbour on the phone—a self-described successful day trader—who admonished me for not having my client buy Nortel stock. "You mean you're telling me that you're not going to tell him to buy Nortel stock!?" he chided.

"That's right," I said, "the stock isn't worth what it's trading for."

"I can't believe that you will not tell him to buy Nortel stock," he said again.

"Well," says I. "Why don't you tell him to buy Nortel stock, and when it goes down then he can complain to you about losing his money."

Such goes the life of an adviser.

There are many different factors that may have affected our personal outcome, such as the timing of when we made the investment, the amounts of capital that we committed, our investment approach and strategies, and how we reacted to our fears during various times throughout the investment period. I have one client who gives me capital to invest only after a significant move up in the market. She's too nervous to add to her position when the markets have been declining, but the bigger the move up, the more money that tends to be given to me to invest. If she gave me the capital when the markets had corrected, her performance would be substantially better, and she hasn't yet been able to understand that larger sums of capital added in later years can distort most forms of performance reporting so when she does her own calculations, she is disappointed.

Our investment objectives and reactions to market events can impact our performance. For example, let's say that you have an objective of minimizing volatility and it's the fall of 2008 and everything is falling apart. Your adviser calls you and says she wants to sell out your equities and move to cash. You agree and are happy when you see your investment fall a further 30 percent from where you sold. You just saved losing another $60,000. Your adviser calls you back in August of 2009 and says she feels that it's safe to head back into the water again. You look at the current price and realize that it is trading 10 percent above what you sold it for.

So, how do you feel about that? In essence, what your adviser did was manage the risk of your portfolio and did so at the expense of your return and to the tune of an "insurance" cost of 10 percent or $20,000. Of course, at the time neither of you knew what the cost of your actions was going to be. If you choose to focus on how you were protected from volatility and from the potential of the global financial system completely imploding, you would be happy that you navigated it correctly. But if you choose to forget all the frightening emotions you were feeling at the time and instead focus on what happened compared to if you had just held, then you would be unhappy.

A Better Way to Look at Things (It All Comes Down to Framing)

Because investment strategies, asset mix, and behavioural issues have such an impact on our investment decisions and performance, let's look at a better way to measure our investment success. Being happy and unstressed is integral to achieving investment success. If we can frame our performance in a manner that lets us see the reality of how we are doing, then we are more likely to stick with a successful program. On the other hand, if we are not doing very well, then perhaps we truly need to change our strategy, or at least understand why we lack success, and we can only do that if our expectations are fair and our results properly measured.

Here are some specific techniques that I use to keep disciplined and to keep the behavioural demons at bay.

Focus on stable features such as dividends rather than unstable features, such as market prices. Back in the old days, before everything was computerized, people held their stock investments in certificate form, usually somewhere safe, like a safety deposit box. By certificate form, I mean that the investor actually had an official piece of paper representing ownership in the number of shares they had purchased. When the investor wanted to sell, he would turn the certificate in to the stockbroker, who would then sell the shares. Those days are long gone, but the psyche behind holding the shares shouldn't be.

Back then, a person holding a collection of shares would have a hard time figuring out what his portfolio was worth. He would have an idea about how each share was doing, perhaps, if he read the quotes in the newspaper, but there wasn't monthly or quarterly reporting from the brokerage firm showing how the value of the entire portfolio was appreciating or declining. The investor was more likely to hold through difficult market conditions because he did not have a value continually telegraphed in his face depressing him every month.

If he held dividend-paying stocks, he would receive his dividend cheques in the mail each quarter, and as time went on those dividends tended to increase. The good feelings that he felt when receiving the dividends positively reinforced his decision to hold the companies that he had. When the businesses increased the dividends they paid him, he would feel even better. Occasionally a company may have reduced its dividend payment, but that was a rare event.

Corporate dividend policy has grown over the centuries and decades from paying out irregular amounts based on current earnings to paying out consistent amounts and increasing those consistent amounts when the company feels they can be sustained.

So, it seems that if a modern-day investor disciplined himself to focus on dividends in such a manner, rather than focusing on the value on his statement every month, the investor would more likely be able to invest as a long-term investor should invest.

Most investors, unfortunately, are not capable of such a discipline. It may be that they have invested in mutual funds and so can't see the dividend specific to their investment, or else they invested in stocks that don't pay a dividend. Further complicating matters, investment and media communities tell them they should "watch" their investments closely and make decisions based on market conditions. Most people have no clue what they are "watching" for and have no clue what they should be doing in any given market condition, and so they fall into the trap of watching portfolio values go up and down and then get scared or greedy and make irrational decisions.

Evaluate how you handled your emotions. Since you aren't likely going to just outright trust a manager or investment adviser without some review, you instead need to train yourself to recognize that when prices are down, a professional manager is making use of the opportunity to improve your future returns. If you are your own manager, then you needed to swallow your fear and embrace the opportunity.

After a market correction, ask yourself if you felt you did the right thing. Ask yourself if you think your decisions and emotions helped or hurt your performance. If you bought in the correction, were you comfortable doing so? Did fear stop you from investing? Be honest with yourself about how you felt emotionally and determine if you are suited for the manner in which you are investing. If not, then you may need to review your strategic asset mix or investment strategy and make changes so that you are comfortable with the risk and volatility you are assuming.

Measure your performance and the success of your strategy over a long period. How should you evaluate or compare how you are doing? The first step is to recognize that you must evaluate from a long-term perspective. The shorter the time frame you use to measure performance, the more likely you are to make decisions incongruent with long-term success.

Proven strategies work over long periods but not necessarily over short ones. I wouldn't measure anything over less than a 3-year period and would rather review how I was doing over rolling 5- and 10-year periods. The advantage of this is that it lets the methods that we are employing have enough time to work.

In his book *What Works on Wall Street*, James O'Shaughnessy introduces the concept of base rates. Base rates are how often a particular strategy outperforms an index or measurement over a given time frame. For example, it may be found that a low price-to-earnings strategy greatly outperformed an index over a 20-year period, but when you look over the 20 years in one-year increments, it may have outperformed in only 12 of the years or 70 percent of the time. If you look at the 16 five-year rolling periods (i.e., you measure five-year average annual growth and can do so from year 5 through year 20), it may be shown that the strategy outperformed on a five-year basis 75 percent of the time. In that regard, you will then be much more mentally prepared to expect that the strategy wouldn't outperform over every five-year period that you may use it. After all, it didn't outperform a quarter of the time. But a 75 percent success rate is still pretty good odds.

Remember Figures 8-1 (B) to 8-3 (B)? If we determine what the base rate was for one-year periods where the market produced a positive return, it works out to about 75 percent of the time. When we looked at market returns over five-year periods, there are 74 positive five-year periods and eight negative five-year periods, so 90 percent of the time the TSX has been positive on a five-year basis. Ten-year base rates are even better, since the TSX has only been negative once on a ten-year basis from 1923 to 2009. Once again, pretty good odds.

This type of longer-term perspective can raise your discipline and your confidence in what to expect.

Measure against realistic benchmarks. Most of us pay fees for the means of our investments, so it is hard to feel good about our investment decisions if we compare our performance to benchmarks that don't factor in all the costs of investing. Peter Lynch felt that do-it-yourselfers need to factor in more than just commission costs. They need to consider the cost of investment research (I spend more than $1,000 per month for investment research) and the cost of their time that they spend in managing their own portfolios. They also need to factor in the cost of getting other advice, such as financial planning and tax advice, which often is provided free of charge to investors with professional advisers. There's nothing wrong with doing it yourself if you enjoy it and are capable of understanding it and have the time to continually keep on top of new tax trends, etc. In fact, there are significant savings that can be had to people who can do it themselves.

Unfortunately, there are also considerable costs when people think they can do it themselves but learn they can't. There is the loss of time for compounding when we don't have a successful discipline in place, there could be an unnecessary loss of capital, and there could be higher tax costs or penalties which arise due to the investor's inability to understand all the tax rules and strategies. Some investors learned this the hard way with their TFSAs recently. Many of these costs are often never known to an investor unless pointed out and quantified by an expert.

There can also be the cost of underperformance caused by an investor's inability to make proper decisions because of behavioural issues or just poor investment decisions and lack of prudence. As the Dalbar studies indicate, the cost to the average investor in the form of lower returns was well above the cost they would have paid for professional and disciplined management and advice.

Real-World Indices

How can we measure performance so that we are comparing our investment experience against real-world results? One solution is to compare your returns against average returns for managed investments with the appropriate asset mix.

For my own use, I've created the *WealthTrust Peer Balanced* and *WealthTrust Peer Growth* indices for just such a purpose. These indices factor in management fees and incorporate different investment styles and diversification, so they give a better perspective of what likely should have happened to my portfolio.

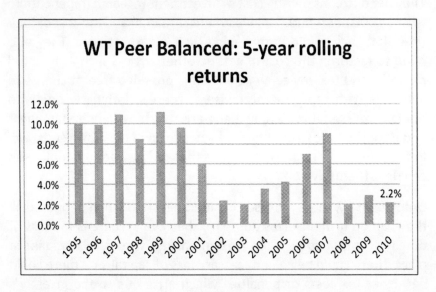

Source: WealthTrust

Figure 8-10 (B)

Measuring the performance of your portfolio against the performance of similar indices, such as those provided by Morningstar, on time frames of five years or longer is a more rational way to determine if your discipline is keeping up with the Joneses. If your performance is not up to snuff, then it's worth the exercise of determining why you have underperformed. Often it will be the result of more conservative or aggressive asset mixes or applying a style that has not been in favour for some time. I've already explained different investment styles and how they have their "day in the sun" at different points in time. That doesn't mean your approach is wrong. It might be perfect for you. The index is only a tool for you to understand what is happening and to determine if changes are necessary.

Why should you be measuring your performance with an index that factors in management fees? Because the objective of investing for most investors should not be to outperform indices, it should be to get positive long-term growth that meets or exceeds your planned rate of return and that represents the risk incurred based on the asset mix that was used.

Would you really be unhappy with a 20-year, 9 percent average annual return when the market did 11 percent, if your target rate was 4 percent? If you are making use of an adviser and professional money managers, they are going to charge you a fee or a commission. In return, you expect advice in deciding on appropriate investments to help you get positive growth and to help you understand your risk tolerances; you are going to want to get comprehensive financial advice, including tax and estate planning solutions to save you money and provide for your loved ones; you are going to want simplification; and you are going to want help in adhering to your chosen discipline. Much of this service is non-quantifiable.

If you are getting 4 percent long-term returns with your adviser when an appropriate index returned 9 percent, then perhaps there is a problem, but without a proper measurement tool you may be passing an unfair judgment on your adviser, and should you change advisers or strategies or decide to do it yourself, you may end up in a worse place.

There's nothing wrong with trying to minimize your investment costs, but realize that if you want to make use of professional help, then your focus should be more on the "value" you are receiving; therefore, the index you use to measure your performance should include fees.

The indices are also useful to those who are not using professional help, because they can better evaluate if their cost savings are worth the extra work involved in managing their own portfolio.

Using a "No-Risk" Benchmark

"I should have bought a GIC!"
O those cursed word
By every adviser heard
After every negative year
We hate them oh so dear

That ditty is attributable to yours truly, thank you very much. That's about the extent of my foray into poetry.

You can also compare your performance against a "no-risk" benchmark such as guaranteed investment rates that existed at the time that you invest. Just make sure that you measure the performance over an appropriate length of time, such as five years, and remember that adding to or taking money from your portfolio will affect your returns.

An example of how to use the GIC rate as a benchmark is as follows: The 5-year GIC rate at December 31, 2005, was 2.9 percent. At the end of December of 2010, the average Guaranteed Investment Certificate (GIC) was yielding 2.1 percent for a 5-year lock up. In simple terms, this will work out to a 10-year average annual return of 2.50 percent with which to compare your portfolio's results. Too many times I've seen investors remember only the higher rates that may have existed at various times throughout the 10 years, even though they likely would not have earned them.

For my own purposes, I have created the *WealthTrust GIC Index*, which approximates the returns an investor would have made if he had adopted a laddered-GIC approach to his entire portfolio. From the chart shown, you can see that a person with a 10-position, 5-year GIC ladder (i.e, so that a GIC is maturing every six months) earned about 2.65 percent from the period 2005 to 2010, which fared better than the *WT Balanced Index* over the same time frame. Of course, this period encompassed one of the worst bear markets in our lifetime, and the outperformance was only by about one half of 1 percent, so a person shouldn't be too upset about underperforming.

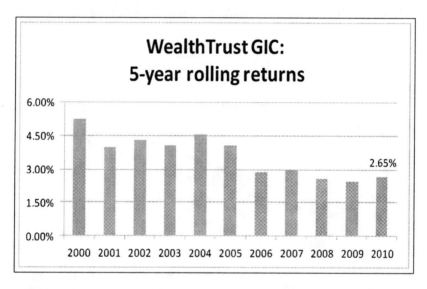

Source: WealthTrust

Figure 8-11 (B)—*a laddered portfolio return for an investment begun in the beginning of 1996.*

Using "Goal-Based" Reporting for Your Target Return—the BAPKIN Way

The target return that I used when preparing my client's planning projection is my preferred performance evaluation tool. This is perhaps the most important measurement of them all because if you fail to achieve this rate of return then you will have to make lifestyle changes such as working longer, saving more, or spending less.

For example, if you have used a targeted 4 percent growth rate for your savings or income requirements when you created your retirement projection, you can measure your progress toward achieving this goal over rolling periods of 3 or more years or you can measure within a target range, say between 2 percent and 6 percent. Should you deviate outside your target range, then you can make adjustments to your plan, such as trying to save more if need be in order to keep your plan on track. The key is that you must be reasonable in your estimates, or your target and projections will be fruitless, and you must do it over longer-term time periods to mitigate the effect of comparing linear projections with variable returns.

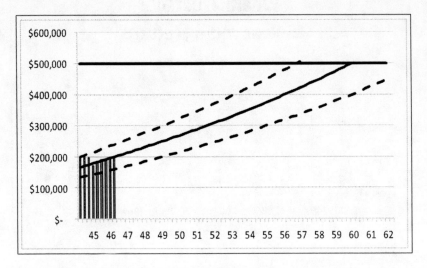

Source: WealthTrust

Figure 8-12 (B)—*an example of using goal-based target ranges when evaluating performance of a portfolio. As long as the portfolio value stays within the range of the upper and lower boundaries, the plan is relatively on track until the later periods.*

PART III: DESSERT (APPENDICES)

As promised, we have some final treats in our BAPKIN Plan. "Part III: Dessert" contains a summary of academic and professional influences that have moulded my investment thinking, a framework for financial decision making, and blank copies of a *Household Balance Sheet*, *Personal Cash Flow statement*, and a *Life Insurance Needs Analysis*, which you can copy and use to determine your needs and monitor your progress.

Appendix 1: Strategies—Academic and Professional Influences

This is a quick rundown on the teachings of some of the more influential academics and money managers so that you can better understand what you are trying to achieve when you invest. My own investing philosophies are based on my analysis of these wise professionals.

Benjamin Graham

Benjamin Graham is considered to be one of the grandfathers of fundamental investing and co-wrote *Security Analysis* (1934) with David Dodd. He also wrote *The Intelligent Investor* (1949). He was an academic and a professional money manager. Graham's approach to investing evolved through the years and much was quantitative and fundamental in nature. Key takeaways from Graham:

- There is a difference between investing and speculating when investing in the stock market. To Graham and Dodd, an investment is one where you have conducted a thorough analysis and expect a reasonable return and the safe return of your capital. Everything else is considered speculation. Having a margin of safety is a key component of an investment.
- Diversification is necessary. Style diversification was the key to his methodology in his earlier years.

- He preferred to invest in companies that had low debt levels and dear valuations.

My take: The importance of style diversification, analysis, and systematic discipline.

James O'Shaughnessy

I consider O'Shaughnessy's book *What Works on Wall Street* to be a great eye opener for investors. He is a professional money manager who offers a number of key lessons:

- A quantitative approach is a passive form of investing.
- Base rates are critical to understand. Base rates are like batting averages and describe how many times the method outperforms the market. If the method outperforms a significant majority of the time, then the investor is likely to stick to the strategy.
- Valuation matters. Low valuation techniques such as price-to-earnings, price-to-cash flow, and price-to-sales vastly outperform indices but can be volatile. It is better if they are used on a combined basis and incorporate a shorter-term relative strength indicator.
- At different times, different value criteria will perform better than other value criteria. They don't always go up and down together for the same periods.

My take: Proven strategies are not always going to outperform even if they do so over the majority of the time tested. Investors have to be prepared that those periods of underperformance may occur, and they would be best served to adopt different styles into their approach to mitigate their wanting to change styles at inopportune times.

Professor Jeremy Siegel

Professor Siegel has written two very influential books, *Stocks for the Long Run* and *The Future for Investors*. The greatest lessons that I have learned from Dr. Siegel:

- Stocks outperform other asset classes when measured over long periods of time.
- It's rewarding if you invest in companies that actually grow their earnings faster over time than what the market expected they were going to grow at. Conversely, we often overpay for stocks that appear to have a fast future growth profile because that growth doesn't pan out as expected. *His basic investment principle is that in the long term, the return on a stock depends on the difference between actual earnings growth and expected earnings growth.*
- This growth trap doesn't just apply to individual stocks but can also apply to sectors of the market and even entire countries.
- Dividends and valuation matter—a lot.
- Having international diversification matters—a lot.

My take: If you are going to invest in companies that appear to be fast growers, you aren't going to be holding them for a long period of time. They aren't necessarily to be avoided, just not bought on a buy-and-hold basis. Stocks that should be bought and held are those where you feel the growth is going to be better than what the market is pricing them at. Also—dividends, diversification, and valuation are important.

Pat Dorsey

Pat is a former director of equity analysis with Morningstar. His book *The Five Rules for Successful Stock Investing* is an excellent primer on Morningstar's approach to security selection. The approach is similar to how I believe Warren Buffet invests. Key lessons:

- Fundamental analysis is the key to selecting securities. Determine intrinsic value by applying a discounted cash flow approach and have a margin of safety for your calculations. He also favours other valuation ratios such as price-to-earnings and price-to-cash flow.

- There's nothing wrong with holding cash until stocks you are interested in buying become cheap enough to provide you with your desired margin of safety.
- Investors best chance to add alpha is by having a behavioural advantage by being more rational.
- Economic moats are important. They represent the strengths that a company has to keep itself profitable amidst a horde of competitive pressures. They can be wide (representing how long their above-average profits can remain sustainable) and they can be deep (representing just how big their profits can be). Ratios that evaluate profitability such as free cash flow, net profit margin, return on equity, and return on total assets help to identify economic moats.
- In the book, he gives a great primer on how to evaluate businesses including looking at growth, profitability, financial strength, risk, and management.
- You should hold for the long term as long as conditions remain positive, but there are times to sell, such as when the stock price has risen too far above your calculated intrinsic value, if the weight represents too large a position in your portfolio, if you have a better place to put your money, or when the fundamentals have deteriorated.

My take: This book is a great read for someone who wants to buy individual stocks or build his or her own portfolio. The importance placed on valuation and moats reminds me that some investment styles are meant for holding investments longer-term while others are meant to hold investments for shorter time frames.

William J. O'Neil

William O'Neil is the co-founder of the daily newspaper *Investors' Business Daily* and has developed the CANSLIM investing system, which he describes in his book *The Successful INVESTOR*. The approach is sales and earnings momentum based, and so it is a refreshing change from the low valuation techniques that others have written about. Key takeaways:

- The direction of the general market matters—it's a lot harder to make money in a falling market, so why bother trying. There's nothing wrong with holding cash while you wait. You want to see a rising market with rising volume—that represents a period of accumulation.
- He believes a portfolio needs to be concentrated, because too many positions are too difficult to follow and it is too hard to react when conditions deteriorate.
- Market technicians only get it right about half the time. Technical indicators are far less accurate than the general market averages.
- Select stocks that represent businesses with very high current and annual earnings, that have a something new about them, that are considered leaders in their industry, that are smaller in capitalization, and that have minimal institutional ownership but that is growing. Buying only takes place when the general market is up and when the stock demonstrates a cup-with-handle breakout pattern.
- You aren't holding for long periods under this methodology. There are different reasons to sell, including if your stock falls 8 percent below your cost or if the price/volume relationship deteriorates.

My take: Fast growers are not meant to be held forever because their growth won't last. Have conditions in your favour before you invest, go with market leaders, and get out when things change.

Peter Lynch

Lynch is best known for his phenomenal managing of Fidelity's Magellan Fund from 1977 until 1990. During that time the fund rose from $18 million in assets to more than $14 billion, with an average annual return of more than 29 percent. *One Up on Wall Street* is one of the best investment books I have ever read. Key investment principles that I have learned from his writings throughout the years include the following:

- How you invest in a stock depends on what type of stock it is. Slow growers, stalwarts, fast growers, cyclicals, turnarounds, and asset plays all have a potential place in a portfolio but you don't buy and sell them using the same criteria, and seldom do you just buy and hold them.
- It's only by sticking to a strategy through the good years and the bad that you'll maximize long-term gains. He didn't like to hold cash and believed that averaging down was a good thing.
- He spread out his holdings mostly between growth stocks and stalwarts.
- Though he owned a significant number of stocks in his portfolio, he believed in concentrated positions as one half of his assets were held in only 7 percent of his positions and 15 percent of his holdings held two thirds of his portfolio.

My take: Different styles of investing will be successful at different times and require different approaches in deciding to buy or sell. A long-term discipline for each style is required to be successful.

Trying to Outperform?

1. You want to invest in equities only if you feel that they will be capable of outperforming guaranteed investments over the time frame that you are concerned about. If the money is to remain invested over a long period, there is significant evidence and rationale supporting the likelihood that equities will outperform guaranteed investments provided that the markets are reasonably valued at the time you make your investment.
2. Stock market indices represent fictitious portfolios comprised of stocks that are included based on criteria such as their size. They do well when money pours into their aggregate components (i.e., the individual stocks that make up the index) and do poorly when money leaves them. So if you want to get returns that approximate those of the index, it's easiest to invest in low-cost products that represent these indices.

3. If you want to try to get returns better than the index, try to buy and sell an index-like investment based on a discipline such as using technical analysis. Even if you don't outperform the index on a straight-up basis, you may find that you do so when you factor in volatility (i.e., on a risk-adjusted basis).
4. If you want to try to get returns better than the index, you can also make use of proven investment styles provided that trading disciplines are followed appropriate to the style. Academics and professionals have demonstrated that both value and growth approaches can outperform indices—for example, the CI Harbour (value) and the Dynamic Power Canadian Growth (growth) are two different style mutual funds that outperformed the Canadian equity index on a 10-year basis as of December 31, 2010. This is not a recommendation to buy these funds. It is merely an observation that different styles are capable of outperforming when a discipline is followed.
5. Different styles have a history of outperforming the market at different times, so diversifying among different styles is appropriate as long as those styles are capable of outperforming on their own merit.
6. If you want to try to get returns better than the index, you can invest part of your equity capital in individual equities that you feel will outperform and the remainder in a low-cost index ETF or mutual fund.
7. There are no guarantees. What worked in the past may not work in the future.

Appendix 2: The Balanced DIET—A Framework for Financial Decision Making and Empowerment

This book was written as a guideline to help those who are not going to get a personal financial plan prepared for them and as a reference guide for those wanting to understand the types of financial decisions they should be making in order to live a better life.

While it would warm my heart to see people carrying my book around in their back pocket the way I see my theatre ad sitting on many tables in a local restaurant after a show, I know it's not a very practical thing.

What I would like to do is to give you a simple framework to help you process any financial decision you may need to make.

The Balanced DIET

There are two things that you will need to remember:

1. *Your overall goal with any financial decision that you make is to increase your assets or decrease your debts.*

    Ask yourself, "Is my decision going to increase my assets or reduce my debts?" If the answer is no, that's cool, as long as you can afford it and it won't upset your BAPKIN planning. If the answer is yes, then that's better, because that's how you grow wealth.

2. *Maintain a balanced DIET.*

So what does DIET stand for? It represents the three key financial stages of your life's journey and includes the overriding cost at each stage—taxes. You should remember that each stage has an overriding objective, and you should ask yourself if your financial decision is moving you toward or away from that objective.

- **Destination**. This is the stage of our journey where we are heading toward our retirement destination. Our overriding objective is to reach our target retirement savings, and our secondary objective is to grow our net worth. This component involves your establishing a target, creating a savings program, concentrating on debt reduction, protecting yourself and your earning power, and investing your savings for growth. Ask yourself, "Will this financial decision help me toward my retirement destination?"

- **Income**. Once you are retired, your financial objectives will be focussed on generating retirement income and reducing the volatility of your investment portfolio. You will need to ask yourself, "Will this financial decision provide me with income to live off, or will it reduce my income—and will I be able to sleep at night regardless of market conditions?"

- **Estate**. In your younger years, life insurance is the solution to creating an estate for your loved ones. As we age we should be focussing on the creation of an estate (in other words, growing our wealth) and then the preservation and distribution of our wealth in an efficient manner, which means with minimal disruption, fees, and taxes. Ask yourself (while you're still of sound mind!) how you want your wealth to be passed to your loved ones, and make sure you talk candidly to a professional to ensure you have structured your will, powers of attorney, and investments in a way that will make things easy and efficient for everyone. *Do this throughout your life's journey and then be sure to keep all the legal documents current—update them every three years*!

- **Taxes**. Throughout our life stages, it should be a goal for us to minimize the taxes that we pay within our accepted risk tolerances and situation in life. Tax minimization should not be a reason for doing something—it should be *one* of the reasons for doing something—but it should also be a factor to always consider.

If you can remember what the main objectives of each component in this acronym are, and you remember to think in terms of increasing assets and decreasing debts, you'll have a good framework to guide you to live a wealthy life.

Household Balance Sheet

Assets - what you own		Liabilities - what you owe	
Current			
Cash and short-term investments	_____	Income taxes payable	_____
Accounts receivable	_____	Credit card balances	_____
Other	_____	Lines of credit	_____
Other	_____	Other loans or debts	_____
Total current	$ _____	Total current	$ _____
Long-term			
RRSP investments	_____	Car loans	_____
TFSA investments	_____	Mortages	_____
Non-registered investments	_____	Investment loans	_____
Life insurance cash value	_____	Other	_____
Total financial	$ _____	Total long-term	$ _____
Principal residence	_____		
Cottage	_____		
Other real estate	_____		
Total real estate	$ _____		
Collectibles	_____		
Other	_____		
Total other	$ _____		
Total assets	$ _____	**Total liabilities**	$ _____
Total net worth	$ _____		

Annual Household Cash Flow

Inflows

Employment income (net)	_____	Alimony	_____
Professional/business income	_____	Child support	_____
Company pension income	_____	Rental income	_____
Old age security	_____	Investment income	_____
Canada Pension	_____	Other	_____
RRIF / RRSP income	_____	Other	_____
	$ _____		$ _____

Total cash inflows $ _____

Outflows

Housing		Transportation	
Mortgage	_____	Lease / loan payments	_____
Rent	_____	Vehicle insurance	_____
Property tax	_____	Gas and oil	_____
Utilities	_____	Maintenance and repairs	_____
Supplies	_____	Parking	_____
Maintenance and repairs	_____	Public transportation	_____
	$ _____		$ _____

Food and clothing		Insurance (excluding auto)	
Groceries	_____	Home/property	_____
Restaurant and entertainment	_____	Life	_____
Clothing	_____	Disability	_____
Other	_____	Critical illness	_____
Other	_____	Long-term disability	_____
	$ _____		$ _____

Debt service		Savings	
Line of credit payments	_____	RRSP contributions	_____
Loan payments	_____	TFSA contributions	_____
Credit card payments	_____	RESP contributions	_____
Other	_____	Non-registered savings	_____
	$ _____		$ _____

Other expenditures			
Education - tuiton, books, etc.	_____	Vacations	_____
Alimony	_____	Donations	_____
Child support	_____	Additional income taxes	_____
	$ _____		$ _____

Total other expenditures $ _____

Total cash outflows $ _____

Excess cash (deficiency) $ _____

The BAPKIN Plan

How much life insurance do you need?

First Capital Pool - cover your current expenses

1. There's administrative costs associated with dying. Funeral costs, legal and excutors fees will add up. $ _____

2. Probate fees are going to range from 0% to 1.5%   _____

3. There will also be income taxes. When you die, it's as if you sold everything for tax purposes, if it isn't transferred to your spouse. Estimate your income taxes that may be incurred - don't forget big items like the cottage.   _____

4. Clear off all your debts. If you haven't utilized your financial institutions' group life insurance for loans and mortgages, then account for them here:

                         Mortgage $
                         Car loan
                         Line of credit   _____

5. Assuming you're a pretty good guy or gal, there's going to be grieving for you. It will be hard for your spouse to work for awhile. Provide some emergency capital for your loved ones to get by on so that they don't have to worry about day-to-day expenses.   _____

Current expense capital required: _____

6. Second Capital Pool - Future expense required - University costs   _____

Total of first and second capital pools: $ _____

225

Total of first and second capital pools: _____

Third Capital Pool - replacing your income

7. Not all expenses will disappear or be reduced if you were to die. Property taxes, heat and hydro are examples of expenses that are not likely to change much, if at all. But food and other expenses are likely to be reduced. Estimate how much income your family will need each month to maintain an appropriate lifestyle (a rule of thumb would be about 40% less than you need now).

            Monthly income $ _____

8. Reduce this amount by your spouse's income   _____

9. This is the net monthly income required   _____

10. Now we have to factor in income taxes. They'll need about 35% more of this income $ _____ - x 1.35 $ _____

11. Assuming your loved ones can earn 2.5% above inflation, divide the required additional income by a factor of .025
Future income capital required: $ _____ / .025 _____

Total capital pool required: $ _____

Where's this money going to come from?

12. You've likely got some sources of capital already squirreled away or established.
(a) Group life insurance through work *** $ _____
(b) Personal life insurance   _____
(c) Cash in your bank accounts including your emergency fund _____
(d) Investments that can be sold or can provide income _____
(e) Registered accounts that will be cashed-in. _____

Total capital that you will already have $ _____

Additional insurance required: $ _____

*** Note: If you are doing this exercise in order to get personal insurance to replace insurance that you have through work then don't include the group insurance in your calculation.

Bibliography

Deans, Thomas William. *Every Family's Business*. Ontario: Detente Financial Corp, 2008.

DALBAR, "Quantitative Analysis of Investor Behaviour (QAIB)" 2005, 2006, 2007, 2008, 2009.

Driscoll, Matt. "Discipline: A Key to Success in Business and Investing." *Tuve Investments Inc.* (2008): http://www.tuveinvestments.com/documents/Disipline-Akeytosuccessinbusinessandinvesting.pdf.

Graham, Benjamin, and Jason Zweig. *The Intelligent Investor*. New York: HarperCollins, 2003.

Graham, Benjamin, David Dodd, Seth Klarmin, James Grant, Bruce Greenwald, and others. *Security Analysis*. New York: McGraw-Hill, 1962.

Gomstyn, Alice. "Finance: Americans Adapt to 'The New Normal'." abcNews. (2009): http://abcnews.go.com/Business/Economy/story?id=7827032&page=1.

Hale, Nathan. "Lessons from a Great Fund Manager's Record." CBS News Interactive. (2010): http://www.cbsnews.com/8301-505123_162-37640453/lessons-from-a-great-fund-managers-record/.

Hood, Duncan. "Retirement: A Number You'll Love." *MoneySense* (2008), February/March: 52–56.

Ibbotson, Roger G., and Paul D. Kaplan. "Does Asset Allocation Policy Explain 40, 90, or 100 Percent of Performance?" *Financial Analysts Journal* (2000) January/February: 26–33.

IE Staff, "Majority of Canadians Nearing Retirement Lack a Financial Plan: Survey," IE Investment Executive. (2011): http://www.investmentexecutive.com/-/majority-of-canadians-nearing-retirement-lack-a-financial-plan-survey.

Leonard, Devin. "The New Abnormal." Bloomberg Businessweek (2010), July 29: http://www.businessweek.com/magazine/content/10_32/b4190050473272.htm?chan=magazine+channel_top+stories.

Lillico, Peter B., Steven C. Bark, Pina Melchionna, and Kathleen Aldridge. *The Estate Planning Toolkit for Business Owners*. Canada: Canadian Institute of Chartered Accountants (2009): 173.

Lynch, Peter, with John Rothchild. *Beating the Street*. New York: Fireside, 1994.

Lynch, Peter, with John Rothchild. *One Up on Wall Street*. New York: Fireside, 2000.

Milevsky, Moshe A., and Alexandra C. Macqueen. *Pensionize Your Nest Egg: How to Use Product Allocation to Create a Guaranteed Income for Life*. Ontario: John Wiley & Sons Canada Ltd., 2010.

O'Shaughnessy, James P. *What Works on Wall Street, Fourth Edition: The Classic Guide to the Best-Performing Investment Strategies of All Time*. New York: McGraw-Hill, 2012.

Russell Investments Canada, "Spending Patterns in Retirement." (2010) February: 1–4.

SEI Investments. "Investing in Canadian Bonds. Research Paper." (1997) February.

Siegel, Jeremy. *Stocks for the Long Run: The Definitive Guide to Financial Market Returns & Long Term Investment Strategies, 4th Edition*. New York: McGraw-Hill, 2008.

Siegel, Jeremy. *The Future for Investors: Why the Tried and the True Triumph Over the Bold and the New.* New York: Crown Business, 2005.

Statistics Canada 89-628-XWE 2007 Number 2.

Statistics Canada. Table 282-0089; Table 280-0017; and Table 280-0008.

TD Bank Group, "Do You Worry about the Unexpected? A Financial Plan Can Help." CNW Newswire. (2011): http://www.newswire.ca/en/story/862127/do-you-worry-about-the-unexpected-a-financial-plan-can-help.

The 2006 Participation and Activity Limitation Survey: Disability in Canada.

The Vanier Institute. "Profiling Canada's Families III." *The Vanier Institute of the Family.* (2004): 83.

Vashisht, Kanupriya. "Market Turmoil Mars Investor Satisfaction, Loyalty." Adviser CA. (2009): http://www.adviser.ca/news/industry-news/market-turmoil-mars-investor-satisfaction-loyalty-20703.

Wyler, Richard G. "Benchmarking Awareness and Attitudes: Survey Shows Top-of-Mind Credentials Are CFP for Millionaire investors, CFA for Financial Advisers." *AIMR Exchange.* (2001) September/October: 12–13.

CPSIA information can be obtained at www.ICGtesting.com
Printed in the USA
LVOW040300011112
305306LV00001B/9/P